WORK WELL

David Westcott *is a director of The Change Partnership and was, until recently, the UK Head of Personnel at KPMG, the world's largest professional services firm. He gained a Diploma in Pastoral Counselling at St John's College, Nottingham, and is a member of the councils of management of The Shaftesbury Society and the Westminster Pastoral Aid Foundation.*

He is a licensed reader in the Church of England and lives in St Albans. David and his wife have four grown-up children.

To Frances

ACKNOWLEDGEMENTS

The author and publisher acknowledge with thanks permission granted to reproduce the following copyright material:

Graham Dow, *A Christian Understanding of Daily Work*. Copyright © Graham Dow 1994. Published by Grove Books Ltd, Ridley Hall Road, Cambridge, CB3 9HV. Reproduced by permission.

Frank Lake, *Clinical Theology*, published and copyright © 1986 by Darton, Longman & Todd Ltd and used by permission of the publishers.

Dorothy L. Sayers, *The Mind of the Maker*. Text © The Trustees of Anthony Fleming Deceased 1941. First published in the Mowbray series 1994, and reproduced with permission of Mowbray, a Cassell imprint.

Scripture quotations taken from the HOLY BIBLE, NEW INTERNATIONAL VERSION. Copyright © 1973, 1978, 1984 by International Bible Society. Used by permission of Hodder & Stoughton Ltd. All rights reserved. 'NIV' is a registered trademark of International Bible Society. UK trademark number 1448790.

Every effort has been made to obtain permission for the copyright material in this book. Omissions or amendments will be made in any reprint.

CONTENTS

FOREWORD

I once knew an economist, with Marxist convictions, who edited a journal called *Zerowork*. His idea of Utopia was a place where work had been abolished.

Many Christians have a sneaking longing for such a place. Their view of work owes more to the Enlightenment, with its separation of sacred and secular, than to the Bible, which teaches the connection between worship and work. Many Christians experience work as a source of stress, insecurity and meaninglessness, leading to that sense of alienation which was described in the Marxist analysis as typical of labour in a capitalist society. This points to a massive failure by the Church – the whole Body of Christ rather than just the officials of the denominations – on two counts. In this book David Westcott addresses both.

Christians urgently need to recover their grasp of and confidence in the Bible's teaching about the place of work in Christian discipleship. The opening chapters of *Work Well: Live Well* provide an excellent foundation for such instruction; in particular, that work must not be defined exclusively as paid employment, important as this is. David Westcott argues persuasively with references and other signposts to prompt further study. It is essential that those responsible for teaching congregations should give priority to reinstating a proper Christian understanding of work. Only then will Christians recover the sense of fulfilment which is God's purpose for His people.

Secondly, he is concerned to provide Christians with the tools to enable us to 'bear one another's burdens'. Although the book, like others in the series, is intended to guide those who regularly engage in pastoral care and counselling, it will be of great value to all who take the responsibility of Christian fellowship seriously. For we are surrounded daily by those who are troubled by problems at work.

The author writes from long experience as a personnel manager in commerce and industry. In this capacity he has had to make hard decisions that cause pain to the individual, but he shows himself to be a sensitive and wise counsellor. He also applies to the book his perspective as an active member of the local church. He is well aware of the apparent ignorance of many Christian leaders of the vital significance of work to the Christian life.

The structure of *Work Well: Live Well* makes it easily accessible to the general Christian reader. Important theological and pastoral issues are placed in the context of a local church and the day-to-day problems faced by its members. David Westcott's vision is that Christians will be equipped to support each other and be more effective as they seek to honour Christ in their daily work. My judgement, as one who regularly meets those who feel wounded by their experience of the world of work, is that this book will help many to bring that vision to reality.

Sir Timothy Hoare

SERIES INTRODUCTION

The demand for pastoral care and counselling in churches has increased to record levels and every indication is that this trend will continue to accelerate. Some churches are fortunate to have ready access to professionally trained and qualified counsellors, but in most situations this onerous task falls to pastors.

Some pastors* are naturally gifted for the ministry of counselling. Some receive training before ordination and then seek to extend this as opportunity permits through the years. Others have the task of counselling thrust upon them. Most seem to feel some sustained demand, internal or external, to be competent in the field. This series aims to address some of the gaps frequently left in theological training. It is intended to offer support to those entrusted with responsibility for the care and well-being of others.

Comparative studies of healing agencies were pioneered in the United States. As long as 30 years ago, The Joint Commission on Mental Illness reported that 40 per cent of 2,460 people canvassed would go first to the clergy with any mental health problem.

Of course there may be reasons other than overtly religious ones for a preference for clergy counselling. There may seem less stigma in seeing a pastor than a psychiatrist. Also, viewing a problem as a primarily spiritual matter may preclude taking some degree of

---

* The term 'pastor' is used generically here, to include all who have a recognized pastoral role within a local church or Christian community.

responsibility for it and for examining its depths. And, of course, clergy visits are cheaper! Unfortunately, there can be the additional reason that parishioners feel an inappropriate right of access to their pastor's time and skills. God's availability at all times is sometimes confused with ours, as is divine omniscience.

Being a front-line mental health worker can put a pastor under enormous and inappropriate strain. Counselling is becoming the primary time consumer in an increasing number of parish ministries.

Feeling unsafe and inadequate in any situation inevitably produces some form of self-protective behaviour, unless we can admit our inadequacy while retaining self-respect. Religious professionals who are under pressure to function as counsellors but know their skills and knowledge to be in other areas may understandably take refuge in various defences, even dogmatism. The term 'religious professional' is more familiar in some countries than in others. The clerical profession actually preceded all others, in status and in time. 'But what are we professional at?' can be a difficult question to answer. This is especially so when clergy are driven to believe that anything short of multi-competence will let God down.

Pastors may feel obliged not to appear inadequate in the area of counselling because of their confidence that the Bible contains the answer to every human need. And it does, conceptually. The difficulty is not with the Bible nor with the pastor's knowledge of the Bible. Neither of these should be in question. The concern is whether pastors have the additional ability of a clinician. Naming a counselling problem correctly – not the presenting problem but the real, underlying issues and their components – is a refined specialism. Making a faulty diagnosis, especially when God and biblical authority are somehow implicated, is the cause of much damage. Clinical terminology can be applied almost at random but with a surprising degree of assurance. Understanding the Bible, and understanding the complexities of clinical practice, are not one and the same skill. In 1985 a comparative study was conducted into the ability of 112 clergy to recognize 13 signs of suicidal tendencies. (Reported in the *Journal of Psychology and Theology*, 1989, Vol. 17, No. 2.) It was found that clergy were unable to recognize these signs any better than educated

lay people and substantially less well than other mental health workers. This is no necessary reflection on the clergy. Why should they be
expected to have this professional ability? Considering them culpable
would only be just if they were to assume, or to allow an assumption
to go unchecked, that their skills were identical to those of other
caring professionals.

One pressure is that graduates of some theological colleges have
actually been taught that ordination will confer counselling skills.
'We must insist upon the idea that every man who has been called
of God into the ministry has been given the basic gifts for . . .
counselling' (Jay Adams, *The Christian Counsellor's Manual*, 1973,
Presbyterian and Reformed Publishing Company, Part One, page 20).

Equating a ministry calling with being a gifted counsellor could be
seen to involve some leaping assumptions. These are becoming more
apparent as we distinguish what we used to call 'the ministry' from
God's calling of *all* believers into ministry. As more work is done on
what we mean by 'ordination' more clergy can be released into those
areas of ministry for which they are clearly gifted and suited.

Belief that counselling skills are divinely bestowed in conjunction
with a ministry 'call' will probably not issue in the purchase of this
series of handbooks! Other pastors who believe or fear that neither
counselling nor any other skills can be taken for granted are possibly
conducting their ministries under some heavy burdens. This series is
written with a concern to address these burdens and to redress some
erroneous equations that relate to them. Each author has extensive
experience in some avenue of ministry and is also trained and experienced in some aspect of counselling.

These Handbooks of Pastoral Care are designed to aid pastors in
assessing the needs of those who come to them for help. The more
accurately this assessment can be made the more confident the pastor
can be about the form of ministry that is required in each instance.
Sometimes pastors will decide to refer the matter elsewhere, but on
other occasions there can be a prayerful assurance in retaining the
counselling role within their own ministry.

Marlene Cohen
Oxford, March 1994

PREFACE

In his biography of the young Martin Luther, Erik Erikson, the distinguished psychoanalyst, observed that he and his fellow analysts had paid little attention to the impact of work on a person's growth and development. He regarded this omission as reprehensible because it neglected a key feature of life. He made good that omission in his biography of Luther, demonstrating the significance of work to the spiritual formation of the great reformer.

The same criticism can be levelled against the publishers of books about pastoral care. Work seldom features, despite the fact that many of us spend a substantial proportion of our time engaged in it. This book attempts to fill that gap, or, if not to fill it, to lay some foundations on which others can build.

At the very outset, I want to comment on three important omissions. First, I say very little about the day-to-day difficulties faced by people who are unemployed, even though I believe unemployment to be one of the worst scourges facing humankind today. My primary emphasis is on those issues we confront while engaged in work, and not on those problems we encounter when we have none. Second, I do not deal at any length with the social, economic, political or other structures within which we conduct our daily activities. While these structures have an enormous impact on the way we live and work, there is very little that can be done by those who offer pastoral care to those who are hurt by them. Third, I do not dwell much on the design of work, other than to observe the dehumanizing effect of the many technological changes that have taken place since the eighteenth century. This crucial topic has already been tackled from a biblical perspective in Christian Schumacher's challenging book, *To Live and Work*.

It will be very obvious to anyone who ventures beyond this preface that I have been influenced chiefly by reading and reflecting on my own experience in industry and commerce. This happens to be my learning style which has stood me in good stead for many years. There are, however, a considerable number of people who have contributed, consciously or otherwise, to the formation of my views. They are too numerous to catalogue here, but I want to mention a handful of companions who have accompanied me on part of my book-writing journey. My two editors, Marlene Cohen and Christine Smith, have provided encouragement when I needed it most. My counselling supervisor, David Charles-Edwards, has helped by drawing on his extensive experience of pastoral care, as has Richard Gill, my dear friend and erstwhile vicar. David Prior, whose ministry focuses on those engaged in the business world, has stimulated my thinking and Tim Hoare, who has helped countless Christians over the years in their choice of work, has graciously added a foreword. Ann Capps has typed and retyped the chapters, making suggestions which I have endeavoured to incorporate. My thanks are extended to these good and patient fellow pilgrims.

My greatest debt of thanks is to my wife, Frances. Throughout our married life she has consistently demonstrated that all work can be God's work. As a mother, a homemaker, an occupational therapist, a school governor, a youth leader and in lots of other roles, she has revealed to me – and to many others – that God can be found in all things; that there need be no distinction between the sacred and the secular; that work and worship are both diminished when separated; and that all people matter because all people are created in the image of God. It is to Frances that I dedicate this book.

Part One

WORKING CHRISTIANS

MEETING THE PROBLEMS

The Pastor's Perspective

Peter looked at his watch again. It was a quarter past eight. Tom had never been late for a meeting before. The others were getting fidgety. The small talk had been exhausted. They were looking purposefully at their papers and at him. 'We'll give it a few more minutes and then we'll make a start,' said Peter. 'Tom must have been delayed at work. It's unlike him to be late.'

Reluctant nods of assent came from the other five people seated at the table. They all knew that it was a bit pointless starting without Tom. He would insist on knowing what had already been decided and would dominate the meeting thereafter. It made sense to wait although it was annoying. Perhaps he won't be able to make it, thought Peter to himself, realizing how uneasy he felt whenever he was with Tom – especially in meetings. He sensed Tom's disapproval. The two of them were of an age, having reached their respective half-centuries within three months of each other earlier in the year. But there the similarity ended. He, Peter, was a vicar whose ministry could best be described as unremarkable. Tom personified success. The managing director of an engineering company, he was the biggest employer for miles around. He was also a good churchwarden – if being a good churchwarden meant running the church as though it were a public company.

How different from Frank, the other churchwarden, who had arrived ten minutes early for the meeting and was sitting quietly in the adjacent seat. Several years older than Peter or Tom, he had taken early retirement from the bank where he had been an assistant manager for a long time. Solid, reliable Frank – he had been a warden longer than Tom but was very much the 'number two' of the pair.

Next to Frank sat Monica. She was there to represent the uniformed organizations – her whole life seemed to revolve around the Guides. She worked in a factory in a nearby town. 'I pack pills' was her standard reply to questions about her job. Alf, her husband, had been unemployed for several years and was seldom seen at church now. Peter worried about Monica's Christian commitment but felt unable to talk to her about her faith, let alone confront her in any way. After all, where would he get another Guide leader if she were to leave?

What a contrast to Nick who was sitting next to her. Peter had watched him blossom and flourish since he had joined the church as a teenager following a local schools mission. Brimming with enthusiasm and energy in everything he did, Nick had followed his father's footsteps into the City after graduating. Peter had been slightly disappointed that he did so. What a loss to the church, thought Peter, he would have made an excellent curate.

Christine was Nick's neighbour. Christine – the very thought of her made Peter wince. He often wished that he had asked his wife, Anne, to interview her before he offered James, her husband, the vacant curacy. Somehow Peter had assumed that Christine would support James in the way that he had been supported throughout his ministry by Anne.

Sadly, this was not the case. When she was not collecting for charity or lobbying the local MP, she seemed to be engaged in a variety of non-church activities and was never available for parish work.

What a difference it would have made if James had married someone like Sally, the last member of the group. In her early 30s with two children, she channelled so much of her energy into the church. She had not gone back to work after the birth of the children, although the family looked as though they could do with some extra money. Indeed, his own wife had once let slip that Sally was having domestic problems but Peter had not pursued the matter further for it was obviously confidential between Sally and Anne. Sally was a gem – always available, always willing to go the extra mile.

Another few minutes passed. All were silent now, lost in their private worlds.

Frank felt empty. He had worked for the bank since he had left school at 15. Admittedly, things had changed a lot in recent years what with mergers, reorganizations and new technology. He had always endeavoured to keep up to date with the latest developments and had prided himself on his understanding of and support for Total Quality Management and Business Process Re-engineering. But he had not reckoned with De-layering and Empowerment. Assistant Managers were no longer required since the bank was becoming leaner and flatter, and junior staff now took on the responsibilities previously discharged by the likes of Frank. He had no choice in the matter. He had been 'offered' early retirement and had received a generous financial settlement. Even though it was now several months back, he could not forget the farewell party which had been a ghastly experience, marked by references to quill pens and dinosaurs. He hated retirement.

Monica did not hate anything – except church meetings. They always made her feel a failure. She had so little to offer and only spoke when the vicar asked her a direct question — which he did slowly and deliberately as though she were a bit slow on the uptake. After all, she was only a production worker at the chemical company. You don't have to be very clever to pack pills. That was how she felt. Why did they ask her to these meetings? She knew she would feel wretched and worthless for the next two or three days and that feeling would not help her to cope with her husband's moods which were becoming ever blacker as each day of unemployment passed.

Nick loved meetings. He loved watching the relationships as first one, then another person tried to get their points across. He loved being involved. In fact, he probably got too involved. That was no bad thing, however. It had been the same at university: secretary to the Christian Union; football in the winter; athletics in the summer; the union bar; the social life; lots of friends. How different from his job in the City! It was positively inhuman looking at a screen all day and communicating by electronic mail. Why had he bowed to the pressure his father had exerted on him? The money and the perks were fantastic, but was it too high a price to pay?

Christine, the curate's wife, was still simmering inside from the row she had had with James that afternoon. He had seen the letter she had received from the international aid agency. They would be delighted to welcome her back to her old job for 15 hours a week. There was a lot going on in the countries she had specialized in and her successor was about to go overseas. Not highly paid, of course, but she would be doing something worthwhile again. Ordination had sounded great when James raised the idea a few years ago. She had a vision of inner-city work, campaigning for the powerless and the marginalized. Moreover, James was stuck in a job he detested. Now the roles were reversed. He seemed to love every minute being in leafy suburbia while she despised the endless round of jumble sales and coffee mornings. And she was going to scream the next time that someone hinted about motherhood. Her thoughts turned to money. How were they going to cope with the debt that was growing bigger all the time? They had long got through their savings. The salary from the charity would at least pay some of the bills.

Sally admired Christine in so many ways. Christine had phoned her that very morning and told her about the job she had been offered. Campaigning for the underdog seemed so much more exciting and important than being at everyone's beck and call. Sally was just like her mother – a veritable Martha. Always available, always willing, always being reminded by the more spiritual members of the church that she was no Mary. How she wished she had the guts to do something worthwhile like Christine.

Peter snapped out of his reverie. 'We really must make a start,' he said. 'We have a lot of business to attend to. It seems as though Tom is not coming. I will get in touch with him tomorrow and explain what we have decided.'

As he spoke, the door opened and Tom entered. His appearance was grim and determined. Peter felt the onrush of uneasiness.

'How good to see you, Tom. We were just about to start. Let us begin with prayer.'

Seven heads bowed.

Tom did not hear the prayer. He had been kept late by the Production Director who had asked to see him after the board meeting. It had been a tense meeting. Sales were down for the fifth month running and there was no sign of an upturn in the market. The bank had refused to increase the borrowing limit. The only solution was to reduce costs which meant laying off about 50 people. The Personnel Manager had prepared a list containing the names of those judged to be the least effective people in the company. A copy of the list had been passed to each of the Directors.

The board had agreed to the list of names by a majority of two. The Production Director was clearly unhappy and Tom was not surprised when he stayed on after the others had left. They had argued long and hard over three of the names on the list. The Production Director wanted exceptions made. He knew the three people well and the difficult personal problems they were already undergoing. Tom had refused to change. The board's decision must be upheld; he would not allow special pleading. They had parted angrily, the Production Director saying something scathing about Tom's Christian compassion. Tom had driven straight from that encounter to the meeting.

Tom had not heard the prayer but the others had ...

> *'Loving Father, be with us as we come together. Help us to lay aside the trials and tribulations of our everyday life. Give us wisdom and strength as we plan to further your work in this place. Amen.'*

Seven heads were raised. Seven pairs of hands shuffled seven sets of agenda papers. The meeting had begun ...

God's Work on the Agenda

It is an imaginary meeting, of course. Peter, Tom and the other characters are not real people. But the thoughts that filled their minds are real issues for many people in our churches today.

There are many Toms: Christian people in senior appointments in business, in central and local government, in schools and in hospitals who have to face up to similar, difficult decisions. Even bishops and clergy are not immune.

There are many Franks who are struggling with the emptiness and meaninglessness resulting from redundancy and so-called early retirement; it seems that no amount of voluntary activity fills the void.

There are many Monicas who lack self-esteem because of the

attitude of their fellow Christians to their job. They are never described as second-rate Christians, but they feel it.

There are many Nicks: young Christian men and women who seriously question whether they are in the right jobs and who struggle on a daily basis with stress, ambition and the insidious growth of material gain.

There are many Christines: Christian women who feel criticized because they do not conform to a particular pattern; and many Sallys, who feel worthless because they do.

Finally, Peter is the Reverend Everyman. The minister who is expected to be leader and servant. The pastor who may have a particular vision but is expected to be all things to all men and all women. The vicar who is having to cope with a level of stress at least as great as that of the others but is not allowed to acknowledge it. All seven characters in our meeting are facing difficulties in their lives which originate in their daily occupations. Stressful work; dissatisfying work; demeaning work; lowly paid work; voluntary work; unacknowledged work; no work – these difficulties, and we could multiply the number many times over, give rise to two major issues. The first of these is pastoral, the second is theological; they are closely related.

Pastoral Issues

These can be highlighted by posing three questions:

- What help can be given to people who face issues similar to those encountered by the characters in the imaginary meeting?
- Who is best placed within our Christian congregation and community to provide that help?
- How are such providers equipped for this particular ministry?

These questions will be addressed later in the book as we explore a range of different situations met in the course of our everyday activities. There are no pat answers for the questions. Though simply stated, they invariably conceal a complicated web of features.

Theological Issues

These matters are theological in nature and concern the meaning of work. We need to address them before we concern ourselves with the pastoral issues, because the manner in which we offer pastoral care to the Toms, Monicas and Sallys will be fundamentally influenced by the views we hold on work. We must, therefore, ask ourselves:

- What is the relationship between God's work and human work?
- Are some occupations more spiritual than others?
- Do some activities honour God more than others?

In many of our churches there is an implicit distinction made between what is described as God's work and the everyday occupations of the church members. Such a distinction was made by Peter when he opened the meeting in prayer. His words were, 'Help us to lay aside the trials and tribulations of our everyday life. Give us wisdom and strength as we plan to further your work in this place.' God's work viewed from this perspective is usually centred on the church and the activities which take place on its premises or under its auspices. The church leadership, in its several forms, co-ordinates and controls the activities in a manner which bears some resemblance to that of other organizations. Church members are usually seen, although not referred to, as the human resources who individually and collectively put these activities into effect.

Most human work which is not church centred is seen to be different. There are honourable exceptions to this rule such as Christian charity workers and those who work for missionary societies. On the whole, however, the two work domains are unconnected. One is sacred, the other secular. One is spiritual, the other worldly.

The Church's Neglect of Work

This might appear an exaggeration, but is it? Reflect for a moment on the emphasis of the public prayers offered in your place of worship over the past months. Consider the time given to those engaged in missionary work, on overseas aid projects, on those training in theological colleges, on young people participating in evangelistic endeavours and on church events. Compare that with the time devoted to Tom's place of work, to Monica's stress, to the tensions facing Nick, to the unaffirmed mothers and homemakers. The balance is almost certainly in favour of the former group.

Consider the following pieces of evidence and match them with that of your own experience:

A 1993 report by the Selly Oak-based organization, Christians in Public Life, showed that while 92 per cent of those questioned by it saw their ordinary work as their Christian vocation and 84 per cent saw their work as part of the mission of the church, only 17 per cent said worship affirmed them in their work to any great extent, only 9 per cent said pastoral care supported them in their work, and only 3 per cent said their local church educational and study programmes addressed their faith and work concerns sufficiently.[1]

In a survey of Christians conducted by Mark Greene, he discovered that 75 per cent of those surveyed had never been asked by their minister about their ministry in the workplace. He also discovered that 50 per cent of that same group had never heard a single sermon on work. Not surprisingly, he concluded that work is not on the church's agenda.[2]

Bishop Graham Dow, when a lecturer at a theological college, asked his new students to write about their former occupations, paying particular emphasis to God's purposes for humankind, the effect of sin on the social aspects of employment and the compatibility between an organization's purpose and the kingdom of God. The reports were almost always of a similar quality and concerned the importance of witnessing to others by conducting themselves with propriety and integrity. He concluded,

> *They did not see that the whole work enterprise belongs to what God has commanded human beings to do in this world. . . they could not see that computer technology or hairdressing or brewing or rolling steel had anything to do with God and his purposes.*[3]

He summarized his views:

> *In work, human beings are to realize their creativity, exercising in unity with others their responsibility as under-managers of God's world. They are to work for the well-being and satisfaction of all, taking delight both in the world God has given, and in the products of their own development of it. Their responsibility is to be drawn out by a close association between their work and their livelihood. They are to worship God offering the product of their work and recognizing the presence of God in all that they do.*[4]

The Consequences of a Different Perspective

The implications of this assertion are far-reaching. We might, for example, start discovering God in the most unlikely places – the factory, the shop, the kitchen, the office. We might also discover that our work takes on an entirely new dimension as we recognize that it is done in partnership with the One whose first recorded activity was the creation of the world. We could find that our spiritual growth is nurtured in the fruitful soil of the trivial round, in the ritual of the common task. We might realize that our so-called 'Christian life' no longer fits uneasily with our everyday life. We might come to see that work – whether it is paid or unpaid, full-time or part-time, in the home or away from it – is part of God's plan for humankind. And if we begin to use this perspective when we encounter the difficulties faced by the Franks and the Monicas and the Sallys in our churches, then the emphasis of our pastoral care is likely to be affected quite markedly. Frank, for example, may feel less empty if we can help him to discover a sense of worth apart from the bank. Monica may no longer see herself as a second-class Christian if we can assist her to recognize the importance of her occupation in the divine plan. Sally may gain a new understanding when she is enabled to find God in everything she does.

All of these conditions – these 'ifs' – depend on our acceptance or denial of Graham Dow's assertion. We are, therefore, faced with two key challenges. The first of these is to question whether his summary represents the view of work contained in the Bible. This we shall explore in chapter two. The second challenge is to discover why, if it is the biblical view, it is not the prevailing one in our churches at the present time. This second challenge will form the subject matter of chapter three. Having looked at these challenges, we can then address those work-related issues which surfaced during the account of that evening meeting.

Part Two

CHRISTIANS AND WORK: BIBLICAL AND HISTORICAL PERSPECTIVES

2

THE BIBLICAL VIEW OF WORK

> ... *it is good and proper for a man to eat and drink, and to find satisfaction in his toilsome labour* ...
>
> (Ecclesiastes 5:18)

What is Work?

Consider for a few moments the following statements:

John is currently out of work.
Jane co-ordinates the youth work at St Matthew's.
I have a lot of work to do in the garden.
The anthem sung by the choir is a lovely work.
Work is a four-letter word.

All five statements are readily understood. They all incorporate the word 'work', yet each statement uses that word in a different way. The first informs us that John has no paid employment. The second refers to Jane's role in her local church. The third identifies a number of tasks such as hedge cutting, lawnmowing and weeding. The fourth describes a musical composition for mixed voices. The fifth is the memorable title of an unmemorable '60s film.

One word with five varieties of meaning ... or six, or seven or more. Clearly we need a common definition before we start to search the scriptures.

A Working Definition

From the many definitions available, I have selected two as being most appropriate to the subject of pastoral care. The first is taken from a dictionary of pastoral theology and the other from a dictionary of pastoral care. The entry from the former defines work as 'human activity designed to accomplish something that is needed.'[1] The other defines it as 'purposeful and indispensable activity to meet human needs and aspirations.'[2]

Three characteristics of work are emphasized in these two definitions. The first is that work involves activity. The second is that the activity has a purpose. The third is that the purposeful activity is essential. Understood in this way, work is demonstrably different from leisure which might share the first two characteristics but not the third. It is different again from rest which is absolutely essential but is characterized by inactivity.

Another feature of these definitions is the implicit inclusion of paid and unpaid work. This inclusiveness enables us to address the topic from the viewpoint of the wage earner as well as from the different – but equally important – perspective of the homemaker, the volunteer and the many others who work without financial compensation. Equipped, then, with this inclusive definition of work as 'essential, purposeful activity', let us start our exploration.

The Approach in Outline

Our exploration will follow along four distinct but closely connected paths and will conclude with a summary.

The first of these paths is the revelation of God himself as a worker. We shall focus initially on the creation account in Genesis before turning elsewhere to discover that God's work can be variously described as creative, sustaining and redemptive.

The second addresses the topic of men and women made in the image of God. We shall see that work is a key feature of the way people reflect and represent God in his world.

The third discusses the consequences of the Fall. Our search will reveal the impact on work arising from 'man's first disobedience' and will recognize the tension that now exists between frustration and satisfaction in work.

The fourth is devoted to Jesus and work. Here we shall observe how Christ, through his incarnation, death and resurrection, facilitates the restoration of the true image of God in those who follow him and, with this restoration, reinforces the fundamental importance of work for those who wish to become like him.

A Working God

God Reveals Himself as a Worker

> *In the beginning, God created ... (Genesis 1:1)*

The very first verse in the Bible tells of God at work, with the remainder of the chapter devoted to the results of that work. The very first verb in the Bible, 'bara' – translated into English as 'created' – describes God's purposeful activity. God's creative work brings forth light and darkness; sea and sky; trees, shrubs and all sorts of vegetation; fish; birds and animals. Finally, he forms men and women as the climax of his creation.

The Trinity Participates in the Work of Creation

John Goldingay, speaking at the Anglican Evangelical Assembly in 1993, made the observation that all three persons of the Trinity engage in the work of creation.[1] God the Father creates. He creates by the spoken Word which, as John's gospel tells us, is the only begotten Son.

And he creates in the presence of the Spirit who hovers over the face of the waters. Father, Son and Holy Spirit are all involved in the work of creation.

God's Work is Good

At each stage of his creative activity, God judges his work to be good. The biblical writer uses no qualifying words to diminish that goodness in any way. God's work is not 'fairly good' nor 'good enough' but 'very good' (Genesis 1:31).

The phrase 'very good' is an interesting one for it can be interpreted in three ways. One way is to construe it in a moral sense meaning that God's work is good and not evil. This is true, of course, but not the connotation here. Another way is to regard it as an aesthetic judgement – that God's created world is a very beautiful one. This, too, is true but misses the real point. The third interpretation is based on an alternative rendering of the Hebrew as 'completely perfect'. This translation is the one chosen by several commentators including Gerhard von Rad, who asserts its appropriateness in the creation account because it places more emphasis on the 'wonderful purposefulness and harmony (of God's work) than on the beauty of the entire cosmos.'[4]

This dual sense of purpose and congruence which characterizes God's work acts as a key feature in our search, for these same characteristics can and do apply to human as well as to divine work. We shall address this when we consider the subject of men and women created in God's image. For the time being, let us simply take note that God's work is good, complete and purposeful.

God's Work Reveals Something of God's Nature

The heavens declare the glory of God:
The skies proclaim the works of his hands.

> *Day after day they pour forth speech;*
> *Night after night they display knowledge.*
> (Psalm 19:1, 2)

This poetic outburst of the psalmist articulates the belief of God's people that God reveals his glory and his nature in the work of his creation. He speaks to the whole of humankind through the created order. It is a view adopted by St Paul in the opening chapter of his letter to the Romans, where he argues that mankind deserves the wrath of God because it has been confronted with a clear picture of God but has chosen to ignore it. The picture he refers to is, of course, the created world in which we live.

Ever since the creation, states the apostle, God's eternal power and his divine nature have been clear for all to see (Romans 1:20). In other words, the world which God has made tells us of who God is. 'Just as artists reveal themselves in what they draw, paint and sculpt,' comments John Stott in his exegesis on this verse, 'so the Divine Artist has revealed himself in his creation.'⁵

This Revelation is Only Partial

This notion of the artist revealing himself in his creation is developed by the novelist and playwright, Dorothy L. Sayers. Using her own experience of writing as a means of understanding God's creative work, she suggests that there are three creative activities which co-exist within the Godhead and which are reflected in human work. She associates each of these creative activities with the persons of the Trinity, which reminds us of John Goldingay's observation referred to earlier. First there is the Creative Idea which is the work of the Father, who conceives the work as a whole from beginning to end. Then there is the Creative Energy, the Son who is present with the Father and embodies the Idea in the incarnation. Third is the Creative Power, the Holy Spirit, who gives meaning to the work. As she develops these themes, she comments:

> *As soon as the mind of the maker has been manifested in a work, a way*
> *of communication is established between other minds and his. That is*

to say, it is possible for a reader, by reading a book, to discover something about the mind of the writer.[6]

The emphasis on 'something' must not be overlooked. The character
of Levin in Tolstoy's *Anna Karenin* is self-confessedly autobiographical,
as is Dickens' character, David Copperfield. We can start to know
Tolstoy through Levin, or Dickens through David Copperfield, yet
we can only know a little for there is far more to both these authors
than is revealed in their novels. Creative work only ever affords us a
glimpse of the creator, a blurred snapshot, as it were. This is as true of
God as it is of men and women. We cannot know God and we cannot
know a human being wholly through his or her work. Our knowledge
is partial. It is incomplete. Yet the fact that men and women, like
God, reveal something of themselves through their work reinforces
the importance of work to humankind.

God Continues His Work

As the Old Testament story unfolds, two further dimensions are
added to God's work of creation. They are the work of sustaining and
redemption. These three dimensions or themes characterize Jesus'
work in the New Testament and set the pattern for human work after
the Fall.

A link between these three themes is to be found in the use of the
Hebrew word 'bara' in the Old Testament. As we have already seen,
it is the very first verb in the Bible and is translated as 'created' in the
opening verse. It is a word which is used exclusively with God as the
subject. The word occurs in many parts of the Old Testament and is a
particular favourite of Isaiah, who uses it more than 20 times. It is to
his prophecy that we will turn in order to see these three features of
God's work.

God's Work as Creator
In Isaiah 40:28, the prophet conducts a court case between the
heathen gods and the God of Israel. His summing up reiterates the

great theological doctrine of creation: 'The Lord is the everlasting God, the creator of the ends of the earth.'

In these few words, the prophet echoes the fundamental belief of the Old Testament writers, that God is the creator and the world is his work.

God's Work as Sustainer

God, however, does not withdraw from his creation but remains involved in the work he has fashioned. For centuries, Christians have used the word 'providence' to describe this involvement. It is not a biblical word but has an unambiguous meaning neatly encapsulated in a collect from the *Book of Common Prayer*: 'Oh God, whose never failing providence ordereth all things in both heaven and earth ...'[7]

Isaiah underlines this divine involvement by expanding the meaning of the word 'bara':

This is what the Lord says —
>   *He who created the heavens and stretched them out,*
>   *Who spread out the earth and all that comes out of it,*
>   *Who gives breath to its people, and life to those who walk on it:*
>   *I, the Lord, have called you in righteousness;*
>   *I will take hold of your hand.*

(Isaiah 42:5, 6)

God the creator works as God the sustainer. 'The heavens are at every moment dependent on the creator to maintain them as his creation,' observes Alec Motyer in his commentary on these verses. 'The power which called everything into being keeps it in being ...'[8]

God's Work as Redeemer

Isaiah 41 contains some exquisite passages of consolation to a dejected Israel and in these we see another development of the word 'bara'. In this chapter God is proclaimed as the One who initiates a great redemption. The creator of verse 20 is the redeemer of verses 14–17, 'transforming his creation (verses 8–19) for the benefit of his needy ones.'[9]

This great redemptive work is most beautifully expressed in the penultimate chapter: 'Behold I will create new heavens and a new earth ... I will create Jerusalem to be a delight and its people a joy' (Isaiah 65:17, 18); and one of the promises contained in this wonderful vision concerns human work: 'My chosen ones will long enjoy the works of their hands ... for they will be a people blessed by the Lord' (Isaiah 65:22, 23).

God's work is creative, sustaining and redemptive. The words capture three themes which permeate the scriptures. Richard Niebuhr is reported as describing these themes as the key biblically derived metaphors for divine activity and human response.[10] They are, in the words of one of Niebuhr's students, 'indispensable for a practical theology of pastoral care orientated towards helping persons discern and respond to the activity of God.'[11] These themes are crucial to our exploration because they form the pattern for all human work. Before we turn to the subject of humankind, however, there is one more observation to be made about God's revelation of himself as a worker.

God Complements Work With Rest

Let us go back once more to the opening chapters of Genesis:

By the seventh day, God finished the work he had been doing: so on the seventh day he rested from all his work. And God blessed the seventh day and made it holy, because on it he rested from all the work of creating that he had done.

(Genesis 2:2, 3)

So ends one of the accounts of creation in the Bible, a story to be taken up again by the same Priestly author in Genesis 5. The passage is so well known that we can easily overlook the significance of it. It is an extraordinary climax to the account of God's creative activity for it ends with rest, a rest that has a number of interesting characteristics.

The first is that it is a rest which follows a completed task. There is no suggestion that God was tired and needed to recuperate. God 'abstained from work and rested', the people of Israel are reminded by Moses (Exodus 31:17), the word signifying that God took refreshment. 'God does not spend the seventh day in exhaustion,' writes Walter Brueggemann, 'but in serenity and peace.'[12] God rested because he had completed what he had set out to do.

The second characteristic is that the day of rest is part of the creation story, meaning that the sixth day is not the end. The six days only make sense when the seventh is introduced. The seventh has no significance without the previous six. Had this early revelation of God been exclusively intended to demonstrate his creative power, the account would have finished on the sixth day. Instead we are presented with a picture of God resting and enjoying what he has made.

The third characteristic is that the pattern of work and rest is here established as the prescriptive pattern for all humankind. God is the divine role model for all to follow: six days of work and one day of rest. The word for rest is the word translated elsewhere as 'sabbath'. This passage in Genesis is not, however, an institutionalizing of the Sabbath. That was to come much later in the history of God's people. This first time of rest is far more significant than an institutionalized Sabbath. It sets the example for all humankind to follow.

God rests from his work, in the presence of his work and in coexistence with his work, concludes Jurgen Moltmann.[13] Patterned on this divine activity, human work and rest are complementary to each other and integrated with each other.

Created in God's Image

Man is Made in the Image Of God

The previous section suggested that human work bears a strong resemblance to divine work. The basis for this occurs in the opening chapters of Genesis. We read that, on the sixth day of creation, God says:

Let us make man in our image, in our likeness, and let them rule over the fish of the sea and the birds of the air, over the livestock, over all the earth, and over all the creatures that move along the ground.

(Genesis 1:26)

As a prelude to developing the theme of the similarity between divine and human work, two linguistic points need clarification.

The first is the word translated 'man'. It is the Hebrew word 'adam' which, in the Old Testament, is occasionally used as a name, more frequently to signify humankind but mostly to distinguish human beings from other creatures. In this particular verse, the use of the word 'them' which follows the first statement makes it absolutely clear that 'man' here means both male and female. As an aside, it seems appropriate for me at this stage to point out that the use of the word 'man' throughout this book should, unless indicated otherwise, be taken to include both male and female.

The second linguistic point concerns the words 'image' and 'likeness'. They are different words in the Hebrew and in our English translations. They have different shades of meaning which cast light on the nature and purpose of work. In the creation narrative they are, to all intents and purposes, synonymous. This becomes clear from an examination of the use of the two words in the early chapters of Genesis. In 1:26 both words are used; in 1:27 only the word 'image'; in 5:1 both occur once more but in the reverse order to 1:26; in 9:6 only the word 'image' occurs. The Orthodox Church, following Irenaeus, insists that the words bear a distinct meaning and develops, from this distinction, a picture of human nature very different from that of the Western Church. The view is an attractive one for those engaged in pastoral counselling and spiritual direction, since it supports the idea of a journey from artlessness to maturity, but it cannot be sustained from this early narrative as it is obvious that the words are used interchangeably.

Having dealt with these linguistic points, let us return to the main issue. What does it mean to be created in God's image and how does the answer affect our understanding of work? We will address these questions by examining the different nuances of the words for 'image' and 'likeness' and then by considering what we know about God from what he has already revealed of himself in the earlier part of the first chapter of Genesis.

Men and Women Resemble God

The Hebrew word for image in Genesis 1 is 'tselem'. The metaphor is that of a carved likeness. Human beings are like God; male and female resemble the Godhead. We noted earlier that the whole of creation communicates something of God's nature. By creating humankind, God reveals even more of himself for God becomes 'visible on earth'.[14] Men and women are, as it were, God's mirror image reflecting the Godhead for all to see. Throughout recorded history, it has been the practice of rulers to display their image throughout their territories in statues, on coins and in objects of veneration. God does not need to do this, which is why he forbids it in the Ten Commandments. Creating a man-made image of God is dishonouring to God for it denies what God has done from the very beginning, namely to create men and women to resemble himself.

Men and Women Represent God

The Hebrew word for likeness is 'demuth'. Whereas 'tselem' suggests resemblance, 'demuth' suggests representation. A representative is one who acts on behalf of another, advancing his or her cause in line with the initiator's instructions. Men and women created in God's likeness are, by definition, God's representatives. Through human beings, 'God works out his purposes on the earth. In us, people should be able to encounter God, to hear his word, and to experience his love. Man is God's representative.'[15]

Like God, Men and Women are Workers

Two conclusions can be drawn from the statement that men and women resemble God and represent God. The first is that it is part of human nature to work, for God reveals himself as a worker and creates men and women to be like himself. The second is that by working in the way God intended, men and women fulfil God's purposes for them. This is what being a representative means, for it involves acting on behalf of and in a similar fashion to the one who charges us with his or her authority.

Man is Different from other Creatures

The difference between men and women on the one hand and the rest of the creation on the other has never been disputed by theologians. The nature of the distinction, however, has provoked much debate and has given rise to a series of views espoused by various theological traditions. Jurgen Moltmann groups these views into four using the word 'analogy' as a means of likening the human to the divine. The four analogies are those of substance, of form, of proportionality and of relationship:

substance: man is different from other creatures because he has an immortal soul which embraces his will and his reason.
form: man is different due to his physical features: the fact that man walks on two legs and gazes upwards demonstrates his distinctiveness from all other animals.
proportionality: a likeness is shown in the dominion that man exercises over the rest of the created order.
relationship: a difference is represented by the way men and women, living in community, reflect the divine Trinity.

Moltmann finds each of these analogies to be insufficient and develops his own view, the full sweep of which need not concern us here. What does concern us is that it includes the assertion that man shows his likeness to God by the very fact that he is a worker.[16]

Human Work is Purposeful and Good like God's Work

The simple statement that men and women are created in God's image attaches 'a manifest value to work', writes Walther Eichrodt.[17] Unlike the myths of other religions which depict the origin of mankind, men and women do not exist for meaningless enjoyment. Quite the reverse, they are 'meant to find the development of their aptitudes and powers in purposeful labour, in which they are to possess a facsimile of the divine work of creation and its joy.'[18] Seen thus, work not only distinguishes human beings from the rest of creation, it is the means by which they exercise their God-given talents and thus fulfil their potential as human beings. A similar view is developed in the Pope's encyclical on work. 'Work,' he claims, 'is the fundamental dimension of man's existence on earth,' through which 'he achieves fulfilment as a human being, and indeed, in a sense, becomes more a human being.'[19] This supports our earlier conclusion that man is able to reveal his humanity through his work.

Men and Women Share in God's Work

Man's work has a purpose, as the creation stories remind us. It includes exercising authority over the rest of the created order (Genesis 1:26, 28; 2:19), and continuing God's work through care and maintenance (Genesis 2:5, 15). By discharging these purposes, man shares in God's creative work and his sustaining work. He becomes God's steward, or as Graham Dow describes it, 'God's undermanager'.[20]

Men and Women Worship God by and through their Work

The scriptural evidence we have addressed thus far makes it clear that work is part of God's plan and purpose for humankind. 'Homo' in the Bible is not just 'Homo sapiens' who is capable of thinking and knowing, but also 'Homo faber' who engages in activities which have a purpose. Work is a key dimension of human existence.

John Stott agrees: it is *a* key dimension but not *the* key dimension of human existence. 'In the end,' he writes, 'a human being is not "Homo faber" but "Homo adorans".'[21] A similar view is put forward by Alan Richardson, a theologian of a different persuasion, who asserts the wholesomeness of work but stresses the greater importance of the Sabbath as the symbol or token of the heavenly rest which all God's people will ultimately enjoy.[22] From yet another tradition, the famous spiritual director, Reginald Somerset Ward, commends a universal Rule of Life which recognizes the importance of work but allocates it to fourth place behind prayer, rest and recreation.[23] These views represent the position taken by many Christians but need to be challenged for they give an inappropriate emphasis and support a distinction between the sacred and secular which is unbiblical. Two key points are overlooked:

Work and Worship

The first point is the separation of work (Homo faber) from worship (Homo adorans) in a way that is unsupported by the scriptures. One of the words for work in the Old Testament is 'avoda', which is sometimes translated as 'work' but also as 'worship'. The reader or writer of Hebrew does not draw a distinction between the two. In the English language the idea which links work and worship is 'service', a word which is widely used to describe our worship on Sundays and which is sometimes used to describe the work which we do on weekdays. Mark Greene makes this connection when he heads a chapter 'Work is a seven letter word' in his book.[24]

Laborare est orare: to work is to pray. The Rule of St Benedict expresses the biblical link simply and directly. Those who adopt the Rule see their work, their worship and their periods of biblical reflection totally integrated in the Opus Dei – the work of God. So, too, did our Celtic forbears whose every activity was immersed in prayer and the worship of God.[25] Brother Lawrence, the French footman turned Carmelite, witnesses to it from his own experience:

> *The time of business does not with me differ from the time of prayer; and in the noise and clutter of my kitchen, while several persons are at the same time calling for different things, I possess God in as great tranquillity as if I were upon my knees at the Blessed Sacrament.*[26]

John Ellerton's hymn captures the unity of work and worship:

> *Thine is the loom, the forge, the mart,*
> *The wealth of land and sea,*
> *The works of science and of art,*
> *Revealed and ruled by thee.*
> *All work is prayer, if it be wrought*
> *As thou wouldst have it done.*
> *And prayer, by thee inspired and taught,*
> *Itself with work is one.*

The separation of work from worship is totally unjustified.

Work and Rest

The second point which is wrongly emphasized concerns the Sabbath. John Stott suggests that the climax of God's work is not the creation of human beings but the institution of the Sabbath; thus inferring that the two events are separate. This, as was demonstrated earlier, is plainly not so. Work and rest in the creation story are integrated – the testimony of Jesus himself confirms it. When criticized for healing an invalid on the Sabbath, he replied to his opponents: 'My Father is always at work to this very day, and I too am working' (John 5:17).

Calvin's comment on this verse is an instructive one: 'the

observance of the Sabbath, so far from interrupting or hindering the course of God's works, actually gives place to them alone.'[27]

The biblical position on this issue can be simply summarized. Just as God's work and God's rest are a unity, so too are man's work and rest, for human beings are created in God's image. Work, worship and rest are inextricably bound together in the scriptures. We should exercise caution when we put asunder that which God has joined together.

Man's Work Involves Relationships

In the second, Yahwist, account of creation, God says: 'It is not good for the man to be alone. I will make a helper suitable for him' (Genesis 2:18).

The words 'not good' contrast dramatically with the Priestly account in the previous chapter in which God declares everything to be 'very good'. It is not, however, a contradiction. The phrase 'not good' is often used in a morally reprehensible way in certain parts of the Old Testament. For example, Ahitophel's advice to Absalom is described in this way (2 Samuel 17:17). Elsewhere it is used as an indication of a state of incompleteness, or a lack of wholesome well-being. Such is the usage in Proverbs 19:2 and in the verse above. Man is incomplete on his own; he needs a helper, a word which – interestingly enough – is used more to refer to God in the Old Testament than to another human being, and in no way describes inferiority or subservience.

If people are to function in the way that God intended, they must be in relationship with each other. This can be seen as reflecting God as Trinity – not separated or isolated, but integrated in unity. We will consider this important feature later, when we see that work which isolates man from his fellow men is 'not good'.

Man's Work Recognizes the Unity of his Being

The Bible emphasizes that human beings are whole people and are not made up of two or more distinctive parts. That this is so is demonstrated by the use of Hebrew words and Greek words when describing men and women. In Hebrew there are four of these words:

'nephesh': often, albeit not always, translated as 'soul'
'ruach': usually rendered as 'spirit'
'lebh': mostly translated as 'heart'
'basar': the 'body', the physical aspects of the person.

In Greek there are five words:

'psyche': translated as 'soul'
'pneuma': translated as 'spirit'
'kardia': translated as 'heart'
'sarx','soma': translated as 'flesh' or 'body'.

In the past, Christian theologians – evangelicals amongst them – have emphasized the distinct parts of the person. The 'dichotomists' distinguished between the body and soul; the 'trichotomists' between body, soul and spirit. Recent writers, however, including those from the evangelical and reformed traditions such as G. C. Berkouwer, George Carey and Anthony Hoekema,[28] have emphasized man's essential unity. The main argument for such unity is a linguistic one. The Hebrew and Greek words can be translated in a particular way but are frequently used interchangeably. Hoekema agrees with the opinion of the Old Testament theologian, H. Wheeler Robinson, that the four Hebrew words 'simply present different aspects of the unity of personality.'[29] A few pages later, he reaches his own conclusion:

> ... man must be understood as a unitary being. He has a physical side
> and a mental or spiritual side, but we must not separate these two ...
> He or she must be seen in his or her totality, not as a composite of

> *different 'parts'. This is the clear teaching of both Old and New Testaments.*[30]

I share this holistic view of man which, as we shall see later, has fundamental implications for the design of work.

The Consequences of the Fall

The Original State of Humankind

Before the Fall, man and woman lived as God intended. Acting together as God's representatives and reflecting his creative energies, they carried out the work entrusted to them by their creator. They were in fellowship with God and enjoyed a mutual intimacy which supported their individuality and their interdependence. They were in harmony with the created order. They were free to choose and were conscious of the consequences of their disobedience.

But they were not in a state of perfection. Theirs was the beginning and not the end of the story. This view combines the position taken both by Irenaeus, whose writings have formed the theology of the Orthodox Church, and Augustine, whose interpretation of the Fall laid the foundation for Catholic and Protestant doctrines. Augustine referred to Adam and Eve in their 'yet to be perfected' state of humanity, implying by this that men and women were still in a state of immaturity. Irenaeus meant much the same when he assumed the parents of the human race were but young creatures with 'unlimited possibilities of growth in God'.[31] Before the Fall, then, the state of humankind was one of sinlessness but not perfection.

The Sinless State is Broken by Disobedience

From that starting point, the question that follows must be: What happens next? We can summarize the familiar story in a few words. The serpent suggests that disobedience is permissible. The woman believes the serpent and encourages the man to participate, which he does. They then recognize what they have done, cover themselves, hide from God and blame others for their actions. As a result, God curses the serpent, punishes the woman, curses the ground and punishes the man (Genesis 3:1–19).

Work is adversely affected by the Fall. In order to assess the extent of this adverse effect, we need to address four themes connected with man's disobedience, namely, damaged relationships, the retained image, common grace and God's covenant.

Man's Relationships are Damaged

Before the Fall, man and woman had a positive and harmonious relationship with God, with each other and with the world in which they lived. Each of these three relationships is changed by the act of disobedience. Direct communion with God is no longer a normal part of the human condition and has to be mediated through sacrifice. Conflict characterizes human intercourse between husband and wife, children and parents, neighbours, colleagues and friends. The environment becomes hostile resulting in a constant struggle often likened to a war. The harmony that once characterized relationships has been replaced by dissonance.

God's Image is Retained

This is clearly shown in the biblical narrative. The author of the first account of creation takes up the story:

When God created man, he made him in the likeness of God. He created them male and female: at the time they were created, he blessed them and called them 'man/adam'. When Adam had lived 130 years he had a son in his own likeness, in his own image and he named him Seth. (Genesis 5:1–3)

From this passage we can see that Seth retained the image of the parents who were created in the image of God. Seth, like the few before him and the millions since, resembles and represents God. All those characteristics of humankind we noted in the previous section are still present in men and women, only now they are affected by sin.

By their act of disobedience, man and woman's resemblance of God is distorted and their capacity to represent God is degraded. God, however, does not cease to love and care for the human race he has created, and this is illustrated in the doctrine of common grace.

God's Common Grace Protects Humankind

The first revelation of God's common grace appears immediately after the account of the Fall. In the story of his making garments of skin for Adam and his wife (Genesis 3:21), we learn of God's protection for his fallen creatures. In the subsequent account of the expulsion from Eden (Genesis 3:23, 24), we recognize God's preventive action to save humankind from what would have been the worst possible fate – that of living estranged from God forever. This theme of common grace which protects men and women from the worst excesses of the Fall recurs from time to time in scripture and is well illustrated in the first chapter of Romans, to which we made reference earlier. We noted that God had revealed himself to humankind through the creation. As Paul develops his arguments he points the finger of condemnation at those who, while recognizing God through his creation, refuse to acknowledge him as such in their lives. This refusal results in God 'giving them over' (translated from the Greek word 'paredoken') to sexual impurity, shameful lusts and a depraved mind (Romans 1:24, 26, 28). The act of abandonment by God implies previous restraint on his part. God, in the words of Charles Hodge, 'withdraws from the wicked the restraints of his providence and grace.'[32] God then continues to provide for his whole creation despite their sin. He also prepares the way for a complete restoration of what men and women were first created to become.

God's Covenant is Announced

This new way is God's redemptive work, that third great theme of his divine activity which is to be reflected in our work. God's common grace is accompanied by God's saving grace. This is prefigured in the early chapters of Genesis and then becomes the great theme permeating the whole of scripture, coming to its fulfilment in the work of Christ. Let us take a brief look at the early manifestation in the story of Noah contained in Genesis, chapters 6–9.

Immediately after the flood, we read of God's new decrees for mankind. Man still bears the image of God (9:6) and acts as God's representative in his work (9:7), although his activities are carried out against a background of strife and violence (9:5, 6). Then we are confronted with a new beginning which is marked by God's covenant in the symbol of the rainbow, a covenant born of his love and affecting the whole of creation. It is made with creation's representative, Noah, a righteous man who walked with God. This first covenant, we may note in passing, is made with someone we would describe as a worker and concerns what we can best describe as creative and sustaining work.

The Impact on Work of the Fall

From the beginning, God's work was very good. Created in his image, human work was also intended to be good. But what do we mean by good work?

Fritz Schumacher, the Christian author of *Small is Beautiful,*[33] suggests that good work should be characterized by a threefold purpose:

> First, to provide necessary goods and services. Second, to enable every one of us to use and thereby perfect our gifts like good stewards. Third, to do so in service to and in co-operation with others.[34]

The Fall has affected this picture of good work in several ways. In the first place, work is not exclusively devoted to necessary goods and services. Envy and greed demand the satisfaction of wants, and wants are seldom satisfied. In Europe, we create mountains of grain and lakes of wine, while much of the world dies of starvation. In our manufacturing plants, we create products designed for obsolescence rather than permanence. In the whole industrial world we confuse creative work with sustaining work. The work of the craftsman, for example, is replaced by the routine machine-based activity and the result is that both lose their meaning.

In the second place, work is not designed to facilitate the development of our gifts. Fritz Schumacher's son, Christian, has demonstrated this very clearly in his book *To Live and Work*.[35] Our failure to design work on the basis of biblical, trinitarian principles has resulted in the deformation of work, which in turn dehumanizes those who have to do it in order to survive.

In the third place, work is not always conducted as a service to others and in co-operation with others. Much work as it exists in developed countries (and, sadly, which has been exported to developing countries) is performed for selfish interests, for our own gratification and to meet our ever enlarging wants. The prevailing ethos is that of competition not co-operation. The language of war is used to describe activities which, in God's plan, should be the language of peace.

The Fall, then, has had a major impact on work. It now has 'the paradoxical connotations of inexorable constraint and joyful expansiveness, unremitting compulsion and liberating self-fulfilment.'[36] This paradox, or rather, this tension, derives from God's common grace which prevents the worst consequences of sin. It can be well illustrated in a biblical case study:

The Pattern of Work After the Fall

This case study is taken from the book of Ecclesiastes, rather than from a selection of passages from the Old and New Testaments for three reasons. Firstly, the writer, Qohelet, reflects on the subject more than any other writer in the Bible. Secondly, he takes a pessimistic, even sceptical, view of life and work. It follows that if a pessimistic, sceptical writer can find something of worth in the subject, it must be worthy indeed! Thirdly, there are numerous points of contact between Ecclesiastes and the early chapters of Genesis, particularly those dealing with the period following the Fall.[37]

At the outset of Ecclesiastes, Qohelet asks a question: 'What does a man gain from all his labour at which he toils under the sun?' (1:3). He then proceeds to give several answers which can be expressed as two statements:

Work does not necessarily give satisfaction if it is viewed exclusively as a means to an end.
Work can give satisfaction when it is viewed as an end in itself.

Let us consider each of these in turn.

The writer has achieved great things in Jerusalem. He has overseen great construction projects and won the respect of the inhabitants. As he reflects on his achievements he comments:

My heart took delight in all my work, and this [the great construction projects] was the reward for all my labour. Yet when I surveyed all that my hands had done and what I had toiled to achieve, everything was meaningless, a chasing after the wind; nothing was gained under the sun. (2:10b–11)

He clearly enjoyed the work itself but not the results he had accomplished (despite their grandeur), nor the respect which had been generated by those results. He describes a similar experience later in the chapter:

For a man may do his work with wisdom, knowledge and skill, and then he must leave all he owns to someone who has not worked for it. This too is meaningless and a great misfortune. What does a man get for all the toil and anxious striving with which he labours under the sun? All his days his work is pain and grief; even at night his mind does not rest. This too is meaningless. (2:21–23)

This time the consequences of the work give him rest-less nights. He has become extremely prosperous as a result of his efforts but he will have to bequeath it to someone else and this gives him no pleasure at all. He does not despair, however, for he has begun to recognize the potential fulfilment which comes from doing work rather than owning the product of work. A few verses later he reflects again:

A man can do nothing better than to eat and drink and find satisfaction in his work. This too, I see, is from the hand of God. (2:24)

Here we see a major shift in his attitude — a realization of the potential satisfaction in work when it is seen as emanating from God. (Reiterated in 3:13, 22.)

Then the writer comes to his final conclusion. Idleness is wrong (4:5), and so is work if the satisfaction which derives from it is motivated by the envy of others (4:4) or the pleasure in producing it is totally self-centred (4:6). But when the attitude is right, then all can be well. Meaning replaces meaninglessness, satisfaction takes over from despair. This is as true of the lowly labourer (5:12) as it is of the rich man:

... when God gives any man wealth and possession, and enables him to enjoy them, to accept this lot and be happy in his work, then this is a gift of God. (5:19)

A gift of God, such as it was in the beginning when he created men and women in his own image. So the pattern established then is still the same despite the Fall. Men and women are still able to find satisfaction and realize their potential as human beings in their work.

Jesus and Work

We now turn to the final path in our exploration, in which we shall discover the potential transformation of human work brought about by the work of Christ.

The previous themes concerning God and work were largely, albeit not exclusively, drawn from the Old Testament. When we turn to the New Testament, we find the same themes recurring in the person and in the achievements of Jesus Christ. We started the first section of the chapter by returning to the beginning, to the creation accounts in Genesis. For this final section, we shall go back to the Incarnation, that pivotal moment in history when God became man.

The Image of God is Revealed

We noted earlier that God has revealed himself in two ways – partially through his creation and more fully in men and women created in his image and likeness. Now, with the Incarnation, God reveals himself fully. 'We have seen his glory,' testified one of his followers (John 1:14), a word which captures 'the attributes of deity showing through the veil of his human nature.'[38]

God became man. He could have come in no other way than to assume human form. He could not have become any other part of creation for no other part was created in his image. C. S. Lewis' 'Aslan' is a fantastic creature of the writer's imagination but it must be confined to fantasy. Allegorically, Aslan can be divine, but not in reality. God became man because only man was created in God's image. In his letter to the Colossians, Paul reproduces a beautiful hymn which echoes the language both of creation in Genesis and Wisdom in Proverbs 22:8: 'He [Christ] is the image of the invisible God'(Colossians 1:15).

The writer to the Hebrews makes a similar claim although he uses a different word. According to this writer, Christ is an 'exact representation of God' (Hebrews 1:3), the word meaning a die or an engraving.

God's image is fully revealed in Christ. He is what God intended men and women to be. Jesus Christ, in George Carey's words, is truly 'Paradigm man'.[39] But he is not only man, he is also God and as such participates in all God's work.

Jesus Shares in God's Creative Work

At the start of his gospel, John echoes the opening verses of Genesis: 'In the beginning was the Word' (1:1).

He then describes how the Word, Jesus, was present with his Father from the beginning, joining with him in creation (1:3).

Jesus Shares in God's Sustaining Work

The theme of Jesus as creator is taken up by Paul in Ephesians and Colossians, making the further point that as well as creating the world, the Son sustains it: 'In him all things hold together'(Colossians 1:17).

This phrase clearly demonstrates that Christ prevents the world from falling into chaos.[40] He is totally involved in God's sustaining work.

Jesus Completes God's Redemptive Work

On four occasions in John's gospel, Jesus talks about accomplishing God's work in a way that is reminiscent of the creation story, but which adds a different emphasis. The emphasis is on redemptive work flowing from God's steadfast covenantal love, which was first revealed in the scriptures in the covenant following the flood.

Jesus introduces his redemptive work early in his ministry when he explains to his disciples that his whole purpose is 'to do the will of him who sent me and to finish his work'(John 4:34). Such a statement undoubtedly bewildered his disciples who, from their response, seem to have had difficulty understanding it. Not long after, he introduces it again. This time it occurs as he explains the testimony which his cousin, John the Baptist, bore to the truth. He applauds John's witness but points to a far greater one which takes place in '... the very work that the Father has given me to finish and which I am doing'(5:36). This work is that of revealing the Father in all his glory, and of showing to the world the love of God by carrying out the work of redemption. It is a work which reaches its culmination in the

Passion and Crucifixion, and is expressed in the great High Priestly prayer recorded in chapter 17. Jesus tells his Father that he has done all that was asked of him. He has indeed revealed God's glory, but not simply by reminding his hearers about God's work from creation onwards. Jesus has revealed God's glory by his life and work. He reveals God's love as he undertakes his great redemptive work. Indeed, almost his last words refer once more to this work: 'It is finished,' he cries (19:30), and his task of redemption is complete.

We are Called to Share in God's Redemptive Work

Just as we are to participate in God's creative and sustaining work, so too we are to share in his redemptive work. We are, as Paul puts it, God's fellow workers (1 Corinthians 3:9). This redemptive work is not only to do with preaching the gospel, although we must never underestimate its importance. It includes all those activities which Jesus modelled during his ministry: feeding the hungry; welcoming the stranger; clothing the poor; tending the sick; visiting those in prison, etc. (Matthew 25:35). It involves healing relationships, reconciling enemies and bringing peace to a troubled world (Matthew 5:9; Ephesians 6:15). It is nothing less than being Christ, the suffering Christ, in the world. We work together with God in all aspects of his work and our work. Creation, sustaining and redemption go together, as Athanasius put it many years ago:

> There is thus no inconsistency between creation and salvation; for the Father has employed the same agent for both works effecting the salvation of the world through the same Word who made it at first.[41]

Jesus Demonstrates the Integration of Work and Rest

We see this illustrated both in the accounts of his earthly life and the task he undertakes after his Ascension.

Let us look briefly at his life. On many occasions in the gospel stories, Jesus is criticized for the way he behaves on the Sabbath. One such criticism is provoked by his healing of the disabled man at the pool called Bethesda (John 5). Because it was the Sabbath, Jesus' critics concluded it was blatantly unlawful. Responding to them, Jesus said: 'My Father is always at his work to this very day, and I, too, am working' (John 5:17).

This angered the religious establishment of the time who, like many today, had split work from worship. Yet it demonstrates unequivocally that the six days of work and the seventh of rest are an integrated whole. Commenting on this verse, B. F. Westcott writes that:

> the rest of God after the creation ... and man's true rest is not a rest from human earthly labour, but a rest for divine heavenly labour ... By the 'work' of the Father we must understand at once the maintenance of the material creation and the redemption and restoration of all things in which the Son co-operated with him.[42]

We see another example of the integration of work and rest in the account of Jesus' activity after the Ascension. Just as God the Father rested when he had finished his work of creation, so God the Son did something similar: 'But when this priest had offered, for all time, one sacrifice for sins, he sat down at the right hand of God' (Hebrews 10:12).

This priest is, of course, Jesus who, unlike the priests of the old covenant offering daily sacrifices (Hebrews 10:11), has 'through his death made a full, perfect and sufficient sacrifice, oblation and satisfaction for the sins of the whole world'. But Jesus, like his Father, does not withdraw from the output of his work at the end of his creative activity. Jesus continues his work of redemption even after his Ascension for now, as Paul assures us, he sits enthroned 'at the right hand of God', carrying out his work of reconciliation by constantly 'interceding for us' (Romans 8:34).

The True Image is Restored

Christ is the perfect image of God and through his work of redemption, we can once more become what God intended. Although this will not be finally achieved until the life to come (1 Corinthians 15:49; Philippians 3:21; 1 John 3:2), there is a sense in which it has already started (2 Corinthians 3:18). It is called the process of sanctification, the work of the Holy Spirit of Christ dwelling within us.

As a result of the Fall, men and women's relationships changed. They became alienated from God, were in contention with each other and at variance with the world that God had created for their enjoyment. Through Christ, the image is in the process of being restored, and with that restoration the relationships which were impaired at the Fall can now be healed. This embraces our relationship to God, to others and to the entire creation. 'The restoration of the image,' writes Anthony Hoekema, 'does not concern only religious piety in the narrow sense or witnessing to people about Christ, or "soul-saving activities"; in its fullest sense it involves the direction of all of life',[3] and that includes work.

This restoration, this transformation of work, can be well illustrated by reference to the observations of a secular writer, Hannah Arendt, whose seminal book *The Human Condition* provoked much debate in the '60s.[4]

In her book, she divided the realm of human activity into three parts – work, labour and action. Work results in artefacts and other products which outlast and transcend the worker. Labour supports the continuous round of growth, metabolism and change which characterizes life itself. Action describes the relationships between people which are essential for their stimulation and growth.

In developing her views, Arendt states that:

> ... *every European language, ancient and modern, contains two etymologically unrelated words for what we have come to think of as the same activity, and retains them in the face of their persistent synonymous usage.*[5]

In English, these two words are 'labour' and 'work'. Their origins are not the same: labour has Latin roots and means toil, trouble and exertion; work is of Northern European stock and originally meant an act or a deed.

The same distinction holds true for the Hebrew of the Old Testament. Two of the words translated variously as work or labour stand in sharp contrast to each other. The words are 'melaka' and 'avoda'. 'Melaka' denotes the creative work of God and his creatures. It is the word used in Genesis 2:2, 3 which tells of God finishing his work of creation. The other word, 'avoda', means the work of a slave. It is this word which is used to describe the activities of the people of Israel when, under a tyrannical and xenophobic pharaoh, they were required to make bricks out of straw (Exodus 5:9, 11, 18).

In the Greek New Testament, a similar distinction is made. Here the two words are 'ergon' (work) and 'kopos' (labour). 'Ergon' is used frequently throughout the septuagint version of the Old Testament to translate the Hebrew word 'melaka'. It is also used throughout John's gospel to define the work of God and of Jesus Christ. In its singular form, 'ergon' bears a positive meaning, although in its plural usage it is almost always associated with evil. The other Greek word is 'kopos', which is usually translated as labour or trouble and is therefore akin to the Hebrew word 'avoda'. In secular Greek the word is usually applied to manual work or sometimes the beating which is administered to a slave.

Work and toil; 'melaka' and 'avoda'; 'ergon' and 'kopos': words in three different languages which describe the wholesomeness of work as God intended it, and its potentially degrading nature as a result of the Fall.

But the Bible does not end with the Fall. Even the most degrading toil can be transformed. We saw it in the case of 'avoda'. 'Avoda' means 'the thankless task of the slave', but through God's grace can mean 'the worship of his people'. We see it again with 'kopos'. 'Kopos' stands for 'toil and trouble' but through Christ it becomes 'devoted service' (1 Corinthians 16:15, 16). The restoration of the image includes the transformation of work.

The Biblical View Summarized

Human work, which reflects God's work, can be conveniently grouped under three headings:

Creative work – to form something of lasting value.
Sustaining work – to maintain that which already exists.
Redemptive work – to heal, reconcile and to repair that which has been broken.

Unlike God's work which is always good, human work can be deflected to evil and destructive ends because of humankind's desire to be like God. Both the conduct and the consequences of the work which we do can be – and often are – negative and destructive. But they need not be so because of God's grace. His common grace allows all men and women to enjoy many of those benefits he conferred on humankind from the beginning. His special grace, mediated through Christ, empowers Christians not only to enjoy those benefits of work, but also to use them in their growth and development as they journey towards the fullness of Christ, the restoration of God's image. For Christians, work has a fourfold purpose:

to glorify God and to worship him
to work with God in conducting his creative, sustaining and redemptive activities
to use to the full the potential with which they have been endowed by God
to serve others by providing for their needs.

In a fallen world these purposes are not easily achieved, for the work of many is degrading, inhuman and meaningless. Yet the possibility to fulfil these purposes is always present, no matter what the task is; for work was and is a gift from God, and work – through Christ – can be transformed into worship and devoted service.

3

A CHANGE IN OUTLOOK

Look to the rock from which you were cut.
(Isaiah 51:1)

Having considered and affirmed Graham Dow's assertion that 'the whole work enterprise belongs to what God has commanded human beings to do in this world', we now turn our attention to *why* this view is not widely held in evangelical circles. Beginning with an historical overview and looking at key themes and events associated with each era, we will consider the impact of these changes on work. We will then examine the variety of responses made by Christians which characterize our attitudes today.

Historical Overview

In this section we shall briefly examine the prevailing views on work held in the Patristic period, the Middle Ages and the Reformation. Then we shall examine in more detail the changes in the eighteenth century which have largely formed our contemporary outlook.

The Patristic Period and the Middle Ages

Opinion is divided amongst historians as to whether the early Fathers and medieval schoolmen endorsed the biblical view of work. Aelred Squire[1] and Matthew Fox,[2] for example, believe that they did. The former draws on Augustine, Ambrose, Benedict and others to make the point that work is God given and to be undertaken for his glory. The latter punctuates his own observations with frequent quotations from Hildegard of Bingen, Meister Eckhart and Thomas Aquinas, encouraging his readers to rediscover a spirituality of work. The basic assumption of Christians in the Middle Ages, asserts Fox, was that work facilitated the worship of God and the spiritual formation of men and women. Aquinas' statement, 'To live well is to work well' is repeatedly used by Fox to underscore the point.[3]

However, theological writers who think that they did not believe the biblical view include A. Marshall[4] and Alister McGrath[5] who both use the fourth-century Eusebius of Caesarea to support their argument. Eusebius, in common with the well-to-do and intelligentsia of his day, dismissed manual work as distasteful and unbecoming for a Christian. It appears, therefore, that opinions at the time were conflicting.

The Reformation

There are no differences of opinion when we get to the Reformation. All historians agree that the Reformers and their immediate successors saw work as an important part of God's plan and the means by which men and women could worship and glorify God. Luther, for example, affirmed that a Christian's vocation was to his or her everyday occupation. As we shall see in chapter five, he was stretching biblical teaching somewhat; such an exaggeration, however, was needed to counter the prevailing view of the time that vocation was something exclusively restricted to a clerical or monastic position. Calvin saw work as 'a dignified and glorious means of praising and affirming God in and through his creation, while adding further to its well-being.'[6] An example of his attitude is shown in his commentary on Matthew 25:14–30, the parable of the talents. Having denied the separability of spiritual from natural gifts, he extends the trading metaphor of the parable to the way Christians should conduct themselves in everyday affairs:

> ... the industry with which each man prosecutes the task laid on him, and his very vocation, the ability to act aright, and the rest of the gifts, are reckoned as merchandise, since their purpose and use is the mutual communication among men. And the fruit of which Christ speaks is the common profit which lightens up the glory of God.[7]

The English Reformers pursued a similar theme, a good illustration being found in the homilies of the Church of England, which were compiled at much the same time as Cranmer's Prayer Book in the middle of the sixteenth century. These compilations of homilies or sermons were published to assist those clergy who 'have not the gift of preaching sufficiently to instruct the people'.[8] One of them is on the subject of idleness, a state of deprivation deplored as much by the Protestant Reformers then as it is by social reformers 400 years later. The author of this homily uses passages from Job, Ecclesiasticus, Proverbs and 2 Thessalonians to reach the conclusion that:

> It is the appointment and will of God, that every man, during the time of this mortal and transitory life, should give himself to some honest and Godly exercise and labour, and everyone follow his own business, and to walk uprightly in his own calling ... which doctrine of St Paul, no doubt is grounded upon the general of God, which is, that every man should labour ...[9]

Although a much more prosaic statement than those of the mystical writers quoted by Fox, it contains the same basic message: men and women glorify God through work. This emphasis was made time and time again by the Puritan divines of the sixteenth and seventeenth centuries, sowing the seeds of what we now refer to as the Protestant work ethic: that whole-hearted commitment to hard work which enables us to honour God. This ethic has survived in various – mostly distorted – forms, but the biblical view of work which preceded it and gave birth to it has not. For between the seventeenth century and the present day we have been subjected to changes which have perverted and deformed the biblical view. Changes such as these, of course, did not happen simultaneously nor exclusively in the eighteenth century, although that era did witness massive shifts which have fundamentally affected the way we live and work.

The Eighteenth Century

A broadly-based summary of these changes seen from a Christian perspective is contained in Karl Barth's work on Protestant theology in the nineteenth century.[10] As a prelude to his evaluatory work, he focuses on the eighteenth century and highlights the following characteristics:

IT WAS AN AGE OF RATIONALISM

One change was the way eighteenth-century people saw themselves in the scheme of things. They discovered a new perspective in comparison to their predecessors, seeing themselves as supremely rational beings with the potential to understand fully the world in which they lived.

IT WAS AN AGE OF COLONIZATION

A second change was the extensive movement of European nations into other countries around the world giving them a sense of superiority and mastery. This was made possible not only by the exploration and trading activities of earlier generations, but by the subjugation of native people and the massive growth of slavery.

IT WAS AN AGE OF SCIENTIFIC PURSUIT

A third change was the consciousness of the power of science and, as a consequence, the power available through science. Every aspect of the natural world, including humankind itself, became a legitimate study of investigation and theorizing.

IT WAS AN AGE OF INVENTION

A fourth change was the invention of machinery which derived from and supported the scientific investigation. It also aided and abetted travel and manufacture. Indeed, the very word 'manufacture' – which literally means 'made by hand' – acquired a new meaning during this period which is still with us today.

IT WAS AN AGE OF POLITICAL UPHEAVAL

A fifth change was a fundamental one in political experience. The end of the eighteenth century witnessed the end of the Holy Roman Empire in Europe, the French Revolution and the American War of Independence. Absolutism of the Emperor or monarch, which had existed in most countries for centuries, was replaced in many by a different sort of absolutism – that of the people being informed and directed by reason.

Of all these changes, two in particular were to have a fundamental impact on living and working; namely, the change in our way of thinking usually referred to as the Enlightenment, and the change in our ways of working which is conveniently described as the Industrial Revolution.

The Enlightenment: New Ways of Thinking

> Eighteenth-century man was the man who could no longer remain ignorant of the significance of the fact that Copernicus and Galileo were right, that this vast and rich earth of his, the theatre of his deeds was not the centre of the universe, but a grain of dust amidst countless others in the universe, and who clearly saw the consequences of all this.[11]

Such is the conclusion reached by Karl Barth. Surely, we might suppose, such a discovery would result in the humbling of man as he realized his insignificance as never before? Not at all, replies Barth, it was quite the reverse. Far from his feeling of little importance, eighteenth-century man felt exalted. The discoveries of Copernicus, Galileo and others were the achievements of human beings acting on their own. It was their investigation, their mental skill which had brought into the open that which had previously been hidden from them. No divine being had revealed it to them; they had found it for themselves. Clearly, they reasoned, the earth was not the centre of the universe. Its place had been taken by another to whom they gave the name 'homo sapiens'. Or, as Barth puts it, the geocentric picture of the universe was replaced by the anthropocentric.[12]

This sea change in the way of thinking was fed by many streams with sources in different places. Two such sprang from the writings of two Englishmen, both of whom died in the first quarter of the eighteenth century and whose work 'created a new mentality among intelligent people, and instantly affected religious thought'[13] – Locke and Newton.

JOHN LOCKE

Two of John Locke's books were to have a profound effect on those who came after him. The earlier and most famous of these was the *Essay concerning human understanding*, published in 1690. All knowledge, according to Locke, is acquired through the senses. Our understanding is formed by what we see, touch, taste, hear and smell. Our reason, therefore, can only operate through our senses. Our beliefs must in turn be subjected to our reason. He proceeded to discuss this in *The reasonableness of Christianity*, where he tackled the question of revelation. He neither doubted the reality of revelation nor its importance to Christianity. On the contrary, he asserted it roundly, concluding that it is entirely compatible with reason. For example, he argued that the world around us demonstrates that its originator must have been wise, loving and powerful. The God who is revealed in the Bible is wise, loving and powerful. QED: revelation is reasonable. Locke, observes Gerald Cragg, 'not only showed how reason functions, he made its role, even in religion, appear inevitable and altogether right.'[14]

ISAAC NEWTON

Isaac Newton asserted that all of nature is governed by cause and effect. This was fundamentally different from the prevalent views of his contemporaries which were based on the assumptions of the medieval schoolmen who, in turn, founded their understanding on the Greek philosophers and the Bible. The pre-Newtonian outlook lay great emphasis on the purpose of the created order – usually known as the teleological view. Newton dismissed this assumption arguing that his universal concept of cause and effect removed the need for any notion of purpose. Nothing more was required. 'To have discovered the cause of something is to have explained it' is the neat summary of Newton's position made by Lesslie Newbigin.[15] The inevitable consequence of this argument was the removal over time of the need to suggest any ultimate purpose at all.

THE SUCCESSORS OF LOCKE AND NEWTON

Both Locke and Newton were godly men. Today we might refer to them as 'committed Christians'. Locke was, in fact, no mean biblical scholar evidencing some of the influence of his Oxford tutor, the Puritan divine, John Owen. Newton went so far as to claim that his great discoveries – the differential calculus, the universal laws of gravity, the properties of light – had all been given to him by the Holy Spirit. But those who followed Locke and Newton and eagerly espoused their rationalistic views did not necessarily share their faith. The overall result was that the supremacy of reason was celebrated, and everything – but everything – became the subject of rational, objective study.

The Industrial Revolution: New Ways of Working

The catalogue of inventions during the eighteenth century is impressive. At the beginning of the century, Hooke invented the optical telegraph and Papin the steam cylinder. Darby's blast furnace was built in 1708. Metal boring machines arrived on the scene in 1720 and accurate spinning machines in 1738. James Watt invented the steam engine in 1764 and patented his condenser three years later. Hargreaves' Spinning Jenny was perfected in 1770 and Crompton's

Mule in 1779. In 1786, gas was first used for lighting purposes.

The rate of change accelerated in the first half of the century and then went flat out during the second half. It was then – 1760 is the date agreed by most modern historians – that the Industrial Revolution started, its birthplace being in England. The range of inventions mentioned above increased production beyond all recognition. Some of this was in response to markets both at home and abroad, with cotton being the classic example of new technology creating a massive, highly profitable market. Some of the increase in production was occasioned by war: for most of the century England was at war with her European neighbours, and in North America and many parts of the growing but vastly dispersed colonies. War demands weaponry and gave rise to more sophisticated metallurgical processes. These in turn were adapted commercially by manufacturing entrepreneurs. The development of the steam engine took place in the mining industry and it was soon adapted for other purposes. The perfection of the steam engine encased in steel and using coal meant that human beings were no longer dependent on natural sources of power. The machine age had arrived.

These inventions only made economic sense (a contemporary phrase not used in the eighteenth century) if they were used on a large scale; large, that is, in comparison with what had hitherto existed. 'Manufactories' – soon to be abbreviated to 'factories' – were built close to the source of the raw materials or the ports into which they were shipped. Transport facilities were improved beyond recognition. Towns were built to accommodate the workers who migrated from the country. The rate of this migration in England was increased by other changes, especially the Enclosure Acts which diminished the amount of common land available and forced people to look elsewhere for their livelihood.

At the beginning of the eighteenth century, the majority of the English population worked on the land, living in small and often inadequate housing. The whole family worked; sowing and harvesting to eke out a basic living. Some might have had an animal or two and made articles for sale or barter.

By the end of the century, a substantial proportion of the

population had removed to the towns, lived once more in inadequate housing and worked in the factories. It represented a change in the pattern of living and working which has lasted until the end of the twentieth century.

The Consequences of Change

The social change happened in fits and starts. Sometimes it was revolutionary; sometimes evolutionary; sometimes seemingly static. Many were caught up in it, but few would have noticed it as dramatically as it is represented in my brief overview, for there was no mass media to inform our ancestors and a century represents three, if not four, generations.

The changes affected work both in the way it was carried out and the way it was viewed. The consequences of these changes are a feature of our inheritance and still influence the way we see things today. We have learned our perspective from the Enlightenment and the Industrial Revolution 'as surely as medieval man was taught his.'[16] Let me highlight a few of these changes.

The Exclusion of God

We have noted the new-found importance afforded to reason in the writings of Locke and Newton. They did not relegate religion to a subordinate position, but saw reason and religion as mutually supportive and necessary. It was not this view, however, that was to prevail in the eighteenth century. Rather it was the philosophy of the French writer, René Descartes, that was to win the day. He claimed:

Our knowledge of both the natural and the supernatural is rooted in human reason; they have a common source and neither has an overriding authority.[17]

Such a notion led easily to the separation of the natural from the supernatural. They were both legitimate subjects for study and, therefore, both subservient to human reason. There was no need to connect them in any way. The understanding of one was neither enriched nor impoverished by an understanding of the other. They were distinct and separate.

Thus it became possible to compartmentalize life in the way that we now know it. Eighteenth-century businessmen could worship in church on Sunday and engage in slave trading for the remainder of the week. Ministers of religion could preach the Kingdom of Heaven from the pulpit and ignore the hell experienced by the members of their congregation who worked in the local factories. Just like the twentieth-century theological students responding to Graham Dow's assignment, which we noted in chapter two, they saw no connection between work and worship. Their views were formed by the mind-set of the eighteenth century and we are their cultural descendants.

The Fragmentation of the Person

The new rational, objective approach extended to the whole of the natural world, animate as well as inanimate. The human being was not exempt. It soon became accepted that if other objects could be disaggregated in order to be understood, so too could men and women. And so began the practice of dividing people into various parts – physical, rational, emotional, etc. This, of course, was not new, because theologians and philosophers had been carrying it out for a long time. Our concern here will be with the theologians.

We saw in the previous chapter that the biblical view of the person is one of wholeness, of essential unity. This became particularly clear when we examined the language of the Old and New Testaments which is unsupportive of any sort of split. But not all Christian teachers have seen it as such. Over the centuries there have been those who have insisted that people are made up of two or three parts. When the split has been taken to an extreme – as in the case of Marcion who asserted that the body was evil – heresy has been pronounced, but for the most part it has been doctrinally acceptable to teach that people are either whole or made up of two or more distinct parts.

The prevailing theological views in the seventeenth century were of wholeness. The reformers, especially Calvin, argued them strongly; the Puritans agreed with him. The writers of the Counter-Reformation (St Ignatius of Loyola and St John of the Cross) concurred. By the nineteenth century, however, the prevailing view – following the influence of the Enlightenment – was that of trichotomy: body, soul and spirit. And while in recent years there has been a marked swing back to a holistic approach, there are still those who affirm the body, soul and spirit fragmentation.

This fragmentation was reflected in the world of work. People were engaged for what they could produce regardless of any other aspect of their humanity. Those who worked in factories were known as 'hands'. Today we pretend to have greater sophistication, talking of 'knowledge-workers' to distinguish them from manual and other workers. Such an attitude was reinforced by the Enlightenment and we are the inheritors of it.

The Devaluing of the Bible

Linked with the exclusion of God and the fragmentation of the person was the subsidiary role afforded to the scriptures. In the seventeenth century, the Bible was regarded as normative and authoritative in matters of faith and behaviour. By the middle of that century, 'Englishmen and women had experienced a quarter of a millennium of emphasis on the sovereignty of the scriptures as the unique source of divine wisdom on all subjects.'[18]

Two things were to change this. The first, as we have already seen, was the replacement of revelation by reason as the ultimate authority. The second was the subjection of the Bible itself to the sort of critical study which was now directed at all other subjects. This criticism, following Descartes' views, started from a position of scepticism.

From 1760 onwards, observes John Kent, 'the classical theologies of Catholicism and Protestantism had to fight for life against wave after wave of criticism both inside and outside organized Christianity.'[19] One outcome was the development of liberal theology associated with the names of Hegel and Feuerbach. Another, according to Max Weber,[20] was the separation in the avowedly Protestant churches of mystery from faith, with the result that the centrality of reason and language in the form of preaching was emphasized at the expense of the sacraments and mysticism.

The revival associated with the name of John Wesley in some ways slowed down this process, but it did not halt it. The gospel he preached gave a message of hope to the hopeless, assuring them of their salvation despite their inhuman surroundings; it provided a message of promise to the able poor who were encouraged to use their talents to their own advancement and the glory of God; it provided a message of challenge to the rich who were asked to care for less fortunate human beings. Wesley's sermons and writings certainly reinstated the Bible as the main determinant of ethical behaviour for some, indeed, for many. But it was only a temporary reinstatement and soon the disconnection of the sacred and the secular was reaffirmed. This disconnection continues to exist today.

The Structure of Work Itself

The new machines of Darby, Arkwright and Watt were designed to speed up the work of the mines and the mills. In some ways, they alleviated the toil and drudgery of factory work. Yet the outcome, dependent wholly on the trading conditions of the time, was either to replace the workers or to make them produce more than ever before. Added to this was the argument of utility. Buying an expensive machine only made sense if there were people in sufficient numbers to mind it – hence the growth of factories. But the designers of the machines now worked on the assumption that human beings could be used to undertake any task, provided it was broken down into its simplest components. And so human beings with all their potential and capability were ignored and the principle of divided labour glorified. The classic illustration of this is in Adam Smith's *The Wealth of Nations*, published in 1776. He describes with approval the new method of making pins:

> *One man draws out the wire, another straightens it, a third cuts it, a fourth points it; a fifth grinds it at the top receiving the head; to make the head requires two or three distinct operations; to put it on is a peculiar business; to whiten the pins is another; it is even a trade by itself to put them into paper; and the important business of making a pin is, in this manner, divided into about 18 distinct operations, which, in some manufactories, are all performed by distinct hands ...*[21]

Such a division of labour increased productivity an hundredfold or even more. The result of this 'economic miracle' was that work itself ceased to have any meaning at all, except as a means to an end. It became an unending cycle of production for the sake of consumption. Men and women became slaves of the machine. The design of work paid no attention to the innate humanity of the person. It ignored 'man made in the image of God', for the designers focused vast expense and care on the inanimate object and none on the person.

Those who work in factories or offices today know that an organization has to comply with ever more rigorous health and safety rules. Dangerous chemicals have to be labelled. Seating positions in front of personal computers have to conform to statutory specifications. These are seen as enlightened practices. And so they are when compared, say, with working practices in the nineteenth century. But they work on exactly the same principle as that established during the Enlightenment – the principle that the essential humanity of the person can be ignored in designing work. This is the tradition we have inherited.

Work and Workers as Commodity

> *... every human being sharing in the production process, even if he or she is only doing the kind of work for which no special training or*

> *qualifications are required, is the real efficient subject in this produc-*
> *tion process, while the whole collection of instruments, no matter how*
> *perfect they may be in themselves, are only a mere instrument subordi-*
> *nate to human labour.*[22]

This simple but profound statement by Pope John Paul II is, as we have seen, the reverse of what has happened. Men and women have become subordinate to the productive output required of them. There is a further aspect of this development which demands our attention. It is that men and women who work in companies have been subordinated to capital. This, too, started in the eighteenth century, although it did not receive its full legal expression in England until the middle of the nineteenth century and later still in other industrial countries. At that time, the limited liability company was formed, which ensured that those who ran companies became exclusively accountable to the shareholders for the effective performance of the company. This is not always the case in other countries but remains so in the UK, USA, Australia and New Zealand. Although not enshrined in law then until a century later, the subordination of labour to capital was established in the eighteenth century – leading to workers being defined as a commodity which could be secured at a particular price in the same way as raw materials. People became the object rather than the subject of work. Their activities were redefined as a commodity.

We still talk of labour markets. We refer to employees as the workforce. People are described in many organizations today as 'human resources'. We are the inheritors of the objectification of work and the worker which started in the eighteenth century.

Women's Work

Historians are divided in their judgement as to whether the Industrial Revolution worked towards the liberation of women or condemned them to greater bondage.[23] Whatever their conclusions, it certainly had an impact:

*In all classes, the eighteenth century reinforced the pattern of the man
at work and the woman at home.*[24]

Prior to the eighteenth century, men and women of what later writers would call the lower-middle and working classes had often carried
out similar work. This was particularly true of those engaged in the
rural economy which was, of course, the majority. Men and women
often worked side by side, equal partners both in prosperity and, far
more frequently, in adversity. Such equality often extended to the
factories and the mines in the early days of industrialization. Women
were engaged as factory hands or as labourers in the pits. Likewise their
children who, when they had lived in the country, had worked in the
fields, now, as town-dwellers, were forced to work in the factories.

As the eighteenth century advanced decade by decade, however,
the situation changed. The invention of labour-saving machinery
resulted in fewer jobs. These tended to be commandeered by the men
who insisted that their womenfolk stay at home. Employers in
England, for example, were obliged to pay poor relief to a man out of
work but not to a woman. Economic advantage therefore led to the
employment of the male at the expense of the female. Gradually but
inexorably women found that their place was in the home bringing up
the children and working to eke out an existence from the pitiful
wage paid to her husband.

It would be entirely wrong to suggest that equality of opportunity
between the sexes existed prior to the eighteenth century. In some
ways, industrialism led to a certain liberalization of women, who were
still regarded as little more than goods and chattels. But the sharp divisions of roles between men and women, particularly in respect of
work, changed radically in the eighteenth century and set a pattern
which, until very recently, has been the norm in industrial society.

The Emergence of the Job

A new word came into prominence after the eighteenth century or,
to be more precise, an old word took on a new meaning. This was the

word 'job'. Before the eighteenth century, the word 'job' was used to describe a particular piece of work to be undertaken, for which the person doing it was usually paid an agreed sum. We still use it in this sense (albeit without the payment) when we talk about the jobs we have to do, for example, over a weekend. We might wash the car, iron the clothes, prune the roses, do the shopping, all of which we describe as jobs. They have no intrinsic relationship to each other. This, then, was the meaning of the word. A person *did* a job – he or she did not *have* a job.

The change in meaning occurred in England in 1780 and up to 50 years later in Western Europe and the USA.[25] From this time, 'job' became something which defined a whole range of tasks undertaken by one or more individuals. Jobs, like every other human activity in the post-Enlightenment age, could now be described, measured, and judged for their worth.

Words often change meaning; however, the changes which occurred to the meaning of 'job' highlight, in an interesting way, the manner in which we have imposed restrictions on the activities which represent work. The emergence of 'the job' imposed new working habits. It created what its nineteenth-century critics called the 'wage slave'. And it introduced a new precariousness into the world of work. The loss of a job would have meant very little in the seventeenth century because it represented just one task. Today, the loss of a job can destroy a person's self-esteem and bring about financial ruin.

Christian Responses

Let us now consider the variety of Christian responses to the changing pattern of work which emerged from the Enlightenment and the Industrial Revolution. In order to do this we need some sort of model, and I have chosen that developed by Richard Niebuhr in his book, *Christ and Culture*.[26] Three factors have influenced my choice of Niebuhr's model:

It has stood the test of time.

It addresses an issue – society – which fits well with the subject of living and working.

It has been used by others to examine and categorize Christian attitudes to other important topics, e.g. Geoffrey Wainwright's writings on worship[27] and spirituality.[28]

Niebuhr introduces five classifications which can be illustrated as five points along a continuum, thus:

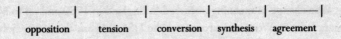

|————|—————|————|————|————|
opposition   tension   conversion   synthesis   agreement

Opposition: Christ against Culture

The attitude at one extreme of the continuum emphasizes an essential antagonism between Christianity and society. It calls on Christians to withdraw from society in order to participate in a wholly spiritual environment. Its rallying call is 'Come out from among them and be separate' (2 Corinthians 6:17). It is the tradition of exclusivism. Niebuhr's examples include Tertullian, aspects of monasticism and certain self-contained sects which were born at the time of the Reformation and still persist today. Writing about spirituality, Wainwright also includes monasticism as an early manifestation of world renunciation and adds Pentecostalism in more recent times.

If we apply this classification to work – but without attempting the historical perspective of Niebuhr or Wainwright – we can recognize an approach which suggests that only certain work is special in God's sight. The phrase 'full-time Christian service' is often used to describe this work. Such a description relegates all other forms of work as being not of God and that, at best, the workplace is a mission field to be evangelized. We saw this view illustrated in the first chapter: the vicar encouraged the other members of the meeting to pray about their forthcoming deliberations because they were all to do with God's work.

This approach is well known in evangelical circles and often takes the form of a spiritual hierarchy of jobs, which has recently been the subject of two books. Mark Greene[29] puts pastors, overseas missionaries and full-time Christian workers at the top of his list; rich Christians and former advertising executives at the bottom. James Allcock's list is shorter – first 'the Church; then medicine; then teaching; then law; and for the morally bankrupt and evil-minded, industrial and commercial life.'[30] The two authors are clearly writing from their own experiences in the advertising world and the gas industry respectively, but many will be familiar with their views.

Agreement: the Christ of Culture

At the other extreme of the continuum is the attitude which suggests a fundamental harmony between Christ's teaching and the ethos of society. Interestingly, this view has been espoused at different times by Christian people of very different social leanings – the radical and the conservative; the democrat and the totalitarian; the revolutionary and the reactionary. Niebuhr suggests Abelard, John Locke and Schleiermacher as examples of Christian writers adopting such a posture. Wainwright adds the Puritan theocracy of New England and, in our own time, the writings of the liberal theologian, Harvey Cox.

Niebuhr describes Christians who hold this position in relation to society as seeing

no great tension between Church and world, social laws and the gospel, the workings of divine grace and human effort, the ethics of salvation and the ethics of social conversation and progress.[31]

Translating this approach for our use, such people see no conflict whatsoever between their faith and the work they undertake. This might be because they see work and worship as inhabiting separate but equally legitimate and compatible domains. Or, on a more positive note, it may include those occupations forming the middle section of Greene's and Allcock's hierarchies, that is, those in the medical and teaching professions. I think it is the view least in evidence among evangelicals.

Having stated the extremes, Niebuhr moves to the more central positions which seek 'to maintain the great differences between the two principles and to hold them together in some unity.'[32]

Synthesis: Christ above Culture

The first of these is to the right of centre (schematically, not politically); it has some affinity to the 'Christ of Culture' (agreement) position but postulates a society greater than humankind can envisage or create by itself. Justin Martyr and Clement of Alexandria from the Fathers; Thomas Aquinas from the Middle Ages, and Joseph Butler in the nineteenth century are Niebuhr's examples. Wainwright gives no additional examples, but points out that the corresponding spirituality is often strongly intellectual or aesthetic.

In terms of attitudes to work, this position is characterized by the recognition of a great potential to be grasped. It accepts that the nature of work is satisfactory to a point but recognizes a greater dimension which can be achieved through Christ. Such an attitude will predispose a person to improve the lot of others through creating better conditions in the workplace; taking more time than is customary with people both to encourage and to help them; acting in such a manner as to raise the tone or standard of behaviour of all. It does not envisage God's kingdom being realized on earth but believes and works towards achieving improvement.

In the foreword to Myron Bush's *Management: A Biblical Approach*, Lorne Sanny writes:

> Drawing timeless principles from the pages of the Bible, Myron presents
> a lively and practical guide for the manager who aspires to greater
> effectiveness and productivity.[33]

This drawing together of the aims of the Christian and the aims of the business in which he or she operates is the attitude of synthesis.

Tension: Christ and Culture in Paradox

To the left of centre is this attitude, which recognizes the tension between two extremes – that is, the existence of two authorities, both of which must be obeyed even though they do not agree. Men and women are seen as citizens of both worlds, which are often in conflict. The best representative of this position is Martin Luther who, according to Niebuhr, 'seems to have a double attitude towards reason and philosophy, towards business and trade, towards religious organization and rites, as well as towards state and politics.'[34] Wainwright concurs, showing that the type of spirituality corresponding to this position is well illustrated by two twentieth-century Lutherans, Dietrich Bonhoeffer and Dag Hammerskjöld. If Paul's phrase, 'Come out from among them and be separate' is the slogan for the first group, those who take this position are likely to plump for John's saying, 'In the world but not of the world'.

People with this attitude towards work recognize that they have to walk a tightrope between two legitimate poles. At one end is the Christian way of life. At the other end is the organization or, more commonly, an individual within the organization who exercises authority. Such authority, according to Romans 13, is derived from God. This can impose dilemmas of an ethical sort which cannot readily be resolved. For the Christian who adopts this approach, the ethos of the organization is important, for he or she is likely to be more comfortable working in a situation where the product or the service is an overtly honourable one. That is why this attitude is positioned on the continuum next to that of Opposition.

The difference is that the range of occupations which such a person can enter is much wider. The key is to be found in the values espoused by the organization. The electrician or the accountant's work is rendered acceptable or not acceptable by the culture and the ethos of the employer. I have encountered it from time to time when interviewing candidates for a Christian charity.

Conversion: Christ, the Transformer of Culture

This attitude is at the centre of Niebuhr's continuum; it recognizes an antagonism between human society and Christianity but believes that a transformation of the former is possible through Christ. Niebuhr's two examples are Augustine and Calvin. Wainwright adds the Franciscans, the Jesuits, the Salvation Army and the liberation theologians of Latin America.

Transferred to work, this attitude is characterized by the belief that although there is often a conflict between faith and work, the latter can be transformed by the former when it is recognized as being part of God's plan for humankind. It finds expression in Thomas Smith's book, *God on the Job*.[35]

This approach is entirely compatible with the biblical view of work we painted in the last chapter. In terms of attitudes to society, it represents the mainstream of Christian tradition, since Niebuhr's champions include Augustine, Calvin and Francis of Assisi.

The equivalent attitude to work was in the mainstream of Christian belief and action until the eighteenth century. It was at the heart of Reformation spirituality, as Alister McGrath points out in his book, *Roots that Refresh*.[36] Sadly,

> *modern Evangelicalism has lost sight of this foundational Reformation insight ... [and] needs to recover the spiritual dignity of work [as] the work ethic has become reduced to 'working for the weekend'.*[37]

Contemporary evangelicals are influenced more by the inheritance bequeathed by the Enlightenment and the Industrial Revolution than that rediscovered at the Reformation. It is this inheritance that influences the distressing range of problems we saw in the fictional account of the church meeting.

Rediscovering an Earlier Perspective

How can we break out of it? The way suggested in this book is to adopt an approach which will be familiar to counsellors pastoring clients who wish to change. It is the approach of re-framing, of taking a new perspective, of creating a new world map. In our case it may mean rediscovering an older rather than a newer version, and recognizing that the one we are using at present has become grossly distorted. As we do this we are likely to become far better equipped to deal with the pastoral problems we saw surfacing at that church meeting. There is even the possibility that some of them, though not all, may no longer be problems. So now, as we revisit the people present at that meeting, let us recall the summary of the biblical view of work at the end of the last chapter, and let us use that view to inform our minds when addressing the issues of our fellow Christians to whom we are providing pastoral care.

Part Three

CHRISTIANS AT WORK: CONFRONTING MAJOR ISSUES

4

THE MOTIVATION TO WORK

Whatever you do, work at it with all your heart, as working for the Lord.
(Colossians 3:23)

Introduction

In this chapter and the six that follow it, I will focus on one of the characters who appeared at that church meeting in chapter one. Those seven people, you will recall, had come together with a common purpose, although we did not learn at the time what that purpose was. What we did discover was that each of them had their own concerns which quickly surfaced when nothing else engaged their attention, and which, for the most part, were unknown to the others.

I will use each of these seven characters as the means of addressing the pastoral care implications of a particular work-related issue. Nick's situation, for example, will serve as the basis for examining job choice and vocation. Monica's story will introduce the subject of stress and Christine's that of self-esteem. Frank's predicament will enable us to explore the subject of loss of work and Sally's circumstances will introduce a debate on women and work.

Two other characters remain: Tom, the churchwarden and Peter, the vicar. Their stories will be told and their situations explored in a slightly different way. I will use Tom as the means of investigating the motivation to work. This is a significant topic for, as we shall see, it links inextricably with views about human nature – a matter on which we touched earlier and one which is fundamental to Christian belief and practice. As for Peter, we will use him when we deal with pastoral care, identifying the range of possibilities open to the local church when helping those who are having difficulties with work.

Before starting with the first character, I want to make a personal point. In my own pastoral encounters with others, I avoid the practice of labelling a person, lest by so doing I identify them with their 'problem'. I would endeavour to meet Christine as Christine, Nick as Nick and Tom as Tom, and accompany them on their journey. In this book, however, I will be using each of the characters as 'case studies', as people with a particular presenting problem. This best serves the purpose of the book, for it allows us to explore the underlying issues and to develop specific strategies for addressing them.

Each chapter will follow a similar three-fold pattern:

1. Colour and substance will be added to the outline of the character sketched in the earlier pages, introducing the 'presenting problem' for our consideration.

2. The particular issue will be investigated, not simply as it appears in the case of the character concerned but in a much broader sense. I will clarify some of the features which might contribute to the problem and will draw on a variety of resources. In the case of motivation, I will refer to the work of business psychologists and management writers. On the subject of stress, I will introduce the views of those engaged in occupational health. The chapter on women and work will cover some of the debates on feminine issues within and outside the Church. All of these themes will be examined in the light of scripture and informed by the biblical view of work developed in chapter two.

3. A variety of strategies to be adopted by the Christian engaged in the work of pastoral care will be set out. The aim of this third part is to give an assortment of approaches from which to choose

when encountering the local equivalents of Sally, Christine and the other characters.

Let us now turn to the first of our new acquaintances, the one who arrived late – Tom, the churchwarden and managing director.

Tom's Story

Tom is 50 years of age. Married to Margaret, they have an adult son who moved to South Africa after graduating as a geologist. He is now enjoying a successful career with one of the multinational mining companies and seldom returns home. Margaret has visited him on several occasions but Tom has done so only once, as the demands of his job make it difficult to get away for long periods. Tom sees a lot of his own career reflected in that of his son, for he himself was based overseas for most of his early working life. It was just about 15 years ago that he returned to the UK, largely as a result of the rapidly deteriorating political situation in the country in which he was working at the time. He was fortunate enough to secure a good position with an engineering company and was promoted to general manager after six years.

Tom and Margaret had taken some time to settle into suburbia after expatriate living and, for a while, Margaret was very depressed. Her salvation, as Tom likes to describe it, came in the form of a neighbour who befriended Margaret and introduced her to a wide circle of acquaintances. Many of these, like the neighbour, worshipped at the local Anglican church and Margaret soon became a regular churchgoer. At first, Tom was reluctant to join her but her gentle encouragement eventually won him over. Tom had always considered himself a Christian and he felt better now that he was a regular church attender.

It was about five years ago that Peter, the vicar, asked him whether he would become churchwarden. Tom was attracted to the idea and assented. Sometimes, he regretted his decision; not long afterwards he was caught up in a management buyout, as a result of which he ceased to be an employee and became a substantial shareholder as well as the managing director of the company. The management buyout completed, Tom and his fellow directors invested heavily in new equipment. The loans stretched the company's resources to the limits, but the investment was beginning to pay off as the order books built up and the market share increased. They even seemed to have overcome the worst aspects of the recession when trouble struck. One of their major customers collapsed, which hit them on two fronts. First, it led to a dramatic reduction in outlets; second, some very large unpaid bills built up.

From that time, things have gone from bad to worse. Each month seems to bring another chapter of gloom and doom. Now they have to embark on a major cost reduction exercise. Tom knows that this is not a sensible long-term decision but they have no choice if the company is to survive.

For Tom, work has always been the most important aspect of his life. He has been highly successful with a whole string of achievements to his credit, of which he is justly proud. He may not have seen as much of his family as he might have done but, as he reminds himself and Margaret from time to time, neither she nor their son have ever wanted for anything. He knows that he is respected by his colleagues and the workforce, a respect built on his hard work, his strong sense of justice and his honesty. All of these, in Tom's view, reflect the outworking of his Christian faith.

Even before the change in the company's fortunes, Tom had become aware of a change in his attitude. He no longer gets a buzz as he drives to the factory – *his* factory as he can properly describe it. He finds himself asking the same questions over and over again: Is it all worth it? What's it all about? Do I really want to carry on like this for another 10 to 15 years? The decision to make people redundant and the Production Director's jibe about his Christian compassion really got to him. He has felt like giving it all up for some time now. This latest episode reinforces that view. He could afford to retire, and Margaret has always said that she would like to see more of him. He has lost interest in his work and has to force himself to do things which, a year or so ago, he would have taken in his stride. Tom is struggling with motivation or – to be more precise – the lack of it.

Motivation

What is it that makes people work? More to the point, what is it that makes some people work harder than others? There is no universally accepted answer to these two questions, although there are any number of theories based – in some instances – on painstaking research. All these theories are influenced, explicitly or implicitly, with the proponent's view of human nature. This link between motivation and beliefs about human nature is a point powerfully illustrated in an observation by the historian, E. P. Thompson. Writing of the changes brought about by the Industrial Revolution, he comments that the severe restructuring of work habits entailed the introduction of 'new incentives and a new human nature upon which these incentives could bite effectively.'[1] Viewed thus, it makes the subject of particular importance to Christians, for it enables us to evaluate each of the approaches in the light of scripture and thereby test their validity. Beliefs about human nature inevitably influence the style adopted by those who manage others, be it in business, in government, at a school or at a church. We shall refer to these styles from time to time whenever an understanding of them might produce some useful clues to the person who is providing pastoral care.

We shall examine five explanations of human nature and motivation; namely, Mechanistic/Economic Man; Social Man; Meeting Man's Needs; Man in Tension; and Developing Man.

Mechanistic/Economic Man

This explanation has a variety of origins – philosophical, pragmatic and scientific.

Adam Smith and Charles Babbage

Philosophically, it owes much to Adam Smith (1723–1790) and Charles Babbage (1792–1871) who propounded the benefits of the division of labour. We have already encountered Adam Smith, whose example of pin-making (taken from his classic work, *The Wealth of Nations*) illustrates the principle perfectly. Charles Babbage took it one stage further. Babbage was a mathematician whose many achievements include the correction and updating of the logarithmic tables, as well as the invention of the calculating machine which laid the foundation for the construction of the modern-day computer. Babbage argued that all human labour should become subservient to the machine, in order that the machine could operate at its greatest effectiveness. For Smith and Babbage the productivity of the machine was more important than the humanity of the operator.

This subservience of people to machines had a long and inglorious history in the nineteenth century, which is vividly portrayed in the so-called industrial novels of Charles Dickens, Benjamin Disraeli, Elizabeth Gaskell and Charles Kingsley. Its widespread practical application came about at the turn of the century.

Henry Ford

For example, it took place in the car industry:

> *The idea that people at work could be treated like machines became popular with employers after Henry Ford opened his first car factory in the early years of the twentieth century and put workers on an assembly line.*[2]

Ford's enormous commercial success was imitated over and over again in many and diverse industries. The assembly line came to epitomize the power of the machine and the meaninglessness of work, finding its greatest artistic expression in Charlie Chaplin's film *Modern Times*.

Frederick William Taylor

It was another American, Frederick William Taylor, who translated Adam Smith's philosophy and Henry Ford's pragmatism into a complex body of knowledge. Taylor is known as the founder of scientific management, a movement which is sometimes referred to as Taylorism. He became 'the first man in history who did not take work for granted but looked at it and studied it.'³ Taylor transformed the principle of dividing work into discrete parts into a sophisticated set of techniques. He introduced what subsequently became known as time and motion study: examining each task; redesigning it so as to achieve the greatest efficiency; and then allocating a time in which to do it.

Completing the task in the time allotted resulted in a basic payment; producing more provided a bonus. His basic assumption was that workmen want high wages more than anything else. From this assumption it followed that the way to improve output was firstly to fragment the task into simple parts, and then to offer financial incentives to those who exceeded the production norms. This was not his only contribution to industrial practices, however. He introduced the distinction between the production workers on the one hand, and those who supervised them on the other. In doing this, he deliberately removed control from the person doing the work – even the most routine work – and passed it to someone else, whose sole task became that of ensuring that others did what was required of them.

Taylor had a clear view about human nature. Allowing for occasional exceptions, he postulated that there are laws of human behaviour which can be verified by observation and used to good effect. His fundamental assertion was that:

> the average workman will work with the greatest satisfaction, both to himself and to his employer, when he is given each day a definite task which he is to perform in a given time and which constitutes a proper

*day's work for a good workman. This furnishes the workman with a
clear-cut standard by which he can, throughout the day, measure his
own progress and the accomplishment of which affords him the greatest
satisfaction.*[4]

J. P. Watson and B. F. Skinner

At much the same time that Taylor was developing his scientific
approach to management, the psychological school of behaviourism
was in its infancy. Here the founding father was J. P. Watson who
reacted against the introspective, analytical approach of Freud.
Watson argued that the study of the mind was unscientific because it
was impossible to see into the mind. A scientific approach, he stated,
must be based on observation and not on subjective interpretations.
The one feature about humankind which can be observed, he
asserted, is its behaviour. This might be the way people speak, their
gestures, postures and specific acts. By observing human behaviour in
all its aspects, it is possible to reach conclusions which can be tested
and verified by others. In Watson's view, all human behaviour could
be explained in terms of stimulus–response associations which are
learned from birth onwards.

B. F. Skinner took these ideas further. He adopted the stimulus-
response concept, but focused on the way the associations between
the two were formed or learned. In time, he gave this mode of learning a name – operant conditioning. In essence, the behaviourist
approach is a reductionist one – it reduces people to a manifold
combination of behaviours, all of which can be observed and understood in the light of prior conditioning. It also suggests that all human
behaviour can be modified by reinforcement and reward.

This emphasis on the person, who is simply a cluster of behaviours, and the power of reward to change those behaviours, is totally
in harmony with Taylorism. As far as we know, Taylor and Skinner
had no contact with each other for at that time, and for several
decades thereafter, there was a mutual distrust between psychologists
and those in business. Yet the fusion of their ideas has influenced the
views of human nature and motivation which are current in many
forms of employment work, and has shaped the style adopted by

those who manage others. Such a view asserts that people work best when they are told precisely what it is they have to do, and goes on to suggest that they will work even harder if there are promised material rewards. Such a philosophy is well illustrated in many of the performance-related pay systems that are adopted in industry and commerce and, increasingly, in public sector and non-profit-making organizations.

At its extreme, this philosophy takes on a particular emphasis characterized as 'Theory X' by the Professor of Management at Massachusetts Institute of Technology, Douglas McGregor. Implicit in the approach of scientific management and behaviourism, argues McGregor, are a number of basic assumptions the main tenets of which are:

The average human being has an inherent dislike of work and will avoid it if he can.

Because of this human characteristic of dislike of work, most people must be coerced, controlled, directed, or threatened with punishment to get them to put forth adequate effort towards the achievement of organizational objectives.

The average human being prefers to be directed, wishes to avoid responsibility, has relatively little ambition, and wants security above all.[5]

There are three criticisms of this view when seen from a Christian perspective:

1. It sees people as fragmented and not as a whole. People become productive units whose task is subservient to that of the machine, the process, the system. No account is taken of the dignity of man and of making him the subject rather than the object of work.

2. It does not recognize human potential. By regulating activities and allowing little or no deviation, it squeezes men and women into a mould which bears no resemblance to the image of God.

3. It panders to man's fallen nature. It rightly recognizes that characteristic in man which is motivated by greed but it mistakenly feeds it. Greed is never satisfied and reward systems built on it inevitably fail.[6]

These beliefs about human nature and motivation result in an autocratic, dictatorial style, frequently caricatured in the media and just as frequently practised in reality.

Social Man

The second approach, prompted by an investigation into the conditions in which people worked, produces a very different view.

Robert Owen, Lord Shaftesbury, the Quakers

The importance of working conditions in factories had long engaged the energies of people working from a humanitarian viewpoint. In the nineteenth century, Robert Owen (the founder of the Co-operative Movement) was the prime mover behind the British Factory Act of 1819. His model factory, schools and schemes of employee welfare attracted enthusiasm and antagonism from within and outside the UK. His socialism and religious scepticism stand in sharp contrast to the attitude of the evangelical social reformer, the seventh Earl of Shaftesbury, yet they were united in their campaign for improvement. Shaftesbury devoted his whole life to ameliorate the lot of those working in 'England's dark, satanic mills'. Still later, and spurred on by both religious and humanitarian motives, Quaker factory owners such as Cadbury and Rowntree made provision for their employees by building schools, hospitals and housing estates. The commercial success of those companies witnessed to the importance of a satisfactory working environment.

Elton Mayo

Armed with the view that the physical conditions in which people work have a positive or negative effect on their productivity, a series of studies was initiated at the Hawthorne (Chicago) plant of the Western Electricity Company, an organization devoted to the manufacture of telephone equipment. At first, the studies were established to investigate the effect of lighting on productivity. The initial findings were totally unexpected. A small group of operators had been separated from the rest of the employees and were observed closely. The first experiment was to improve the lighting. The result of this was that productivity increased. The lighting levels were then lowered. To the surprise of the researchers, productivity improved once more. Indeed, whatever changes were made to the working environment, there was a continual increase in output. Soon, it became clear that the original objectives of the research had to be redefined. For the next five years (1927–1932) and under the leadership of Elton Mayo, a whole range of studies were completed. The findings became the foundation of what is often called the Human Relations Movement. Three key findings stand out above the rest:

1. The effects of financial incentives on industrial productivity were very limited.

2. The social aspects of work were of paramount importance to all employees.

3. Bafflingly, work groups maintained an informal norm of output, which largely fixed output at a constant level, regardless of physical conditions or managerial interventions.

This Human Relations School stresses the importance of positive, constructive social relationships at work. It operates on the assumption that human beings are essentially social, with an innate desire to co-operate and thereby discover their identity through relationships. There are some points about this approach which accord well with scripture and others which do not.

First, the stress on social relationships accords well with the biblical teaching on human nature. 'It is not good for man to be alone,' said God (Genesis 2:18). Second, it separates people between those who work and those who supervise them in such a way as to deny the inherent dignity of humankind. Mayo and his followers saw 'ordinary' employees as governed by a 'logic of sentiment' and managers as driven by a rational appraisal of the situation.[7] This provides little opportunity for personal growth and development. Third, it pays little attention to the work itself, which ceases to have any intrinsic meaning – a far cry from those creative and sustaining features which should be the hallmark of human work.

Managers who adopt this approach give great emphasis to the importance of the group, sometimes to the detriment of achieving the task. We see some revival of this view in the considerable emphasis given to teamwork and team membership in the 1990s.

The third approach recognizes the importance of working with people but sees it as only one aspect among others. I have termed it:

Meeting Man's Needs

So far I have made no mention of the obvious fact that men and women work because they need to work. It has been an implicit rather than an explicit assumption. We will now look at the work of two influential writers who have concentrated explicitly on human needs in their theories of motivation: David McClelland and Abraham Maslow.

David McClelland

McClelland's *magnum opus*, *Human Motivation*[8] contains the fruit of forty years' study on the subject and cannot be easily summarized in a few sentences. His canvas is broad, for he examines individuals, groups, organizations and societies. His sources are diverse, drawing on the research of biologists, anthropologists, educationalists, historians and many others outside his own sphere of social and behavioural science.

From his extensive studies, his categorization of four sets of needs or motives is one which can be most readily presented and is also of most value to our own work. These four groupings are largely self-explanatory and call for little by way of exposition:

THE NEED FOR ACHIEVEMENT
This is the innate drive which motivates people towards success in attaining the objectives set for them by themselves, by others or by society.

THE NEED FOR POWER
This is that characteristic of humankind which wants to control and dominate, be it other people or the environment in which they are placed.

THE NEED FOR AFFILIATION
McClelland groups together the desires for relationships with others, for love and for caring support.

THE NEED FOR AVOIDANCE
This includes those efforts to avoid pain and fear as well as those which reduce anxiety.

Because of his emphasis on the context in which a task is to be performed, as well as the personality characteristic of the individual, McClelland's work has been used in a predictive sense. Tests have been derived from it which measure the particular strength of an individual configuration of needs. Armed with this information, it is possible – so the argument goes – to predict how a person might act in any particular role. McClelland's synthesis of much of the work done by others, together with his own, is a valuable alternative to the earlier two approaches which focused on only one aspect.

His views on human nature are less easy to discover and have to be inferred from his writings. He appears to share the deterministic stance of the classical analysts and behaviourists. That view suggests that our behaviour is the subject of forces over which we have no initial control, indeed, we may never have any control over it. For example, the manner in which we are brought up and educated will determine the degree of trust we have in others, our autonomy, etc. The norms of the society in which we live will have their own separate influence, leaving us feeling powerless.

Such views contain an element of Christian truth but lack two important factors. First, they do not recognize the tension which exists in human nature on account of the Fall, a tension which is captured by St Paul's 'for what I do is not the good I want to do; no, the evil I do not want to do – this I keep on doing' (Romans 7:19). Second, and linked to it, is that it does not acknowledge free will. The person seen from a deterministic viewpoint, who is totally formed by people, events and society, bears only a passing resemblance to the biblical view of man, made by God as 'a little lower than the heavenly beings', made to rule 'over the works of [God's] hands' (Psalm 8:5, 6).

Abraham Maslow

Maslow took the insights of Mayo, as well as those of the analysts and the behaviourists, and evolved his own synthesis, which is described in his influential publication *Motivation and Personality*.[9] In this book, Maslow asserted that the manner in which work was organized in US companies (and the same could have been written about other industrialized countries) deprived workers from the opportunity of gaining any sort of satisfaction from their work. The behaviourist notion that financial incentives were the key to increased productivity was narrow and unsustainable. Such an approach, he argued, dealt only with people's basic needs and failed to recognize that 'the individual is an integrated, organized whole.'[10] In asserting this, he dismissed the underlying proposition that humankind can be fragmented so that a person can be regarded as a 'hand' or a 'mind', separate from the rest of his or her being. 'It is John Smith who works,' he wrote, 'not John's stomach.'[11] So what did he put forward as an alternative to the prevailing models? He suggested an hierarchy of needs, the satisfaction of which forms the basis of the person's motivation. Once a lower level on that scale has been satisfied, he contended, a new set becomes apparent and calls out for satisfaction. A brief summary of his hierarchy will illustrate his views. The basic needs he called:

PHYSIOLOGICAL

These are the needs of survival: for food, for drink, for warmth. A person deprived of these will be strongly motivated by their acquisition. To the hungry person, Utopia is a place of unlimited food, the attainment of which will be all-consuming. Once satisfied, however, these needs are no longer the driving force they once were; other needs become apparent, for example:

SAFETY

These are the needs of protection, of security, of freedom from fear and anxiety. Such needs impact on the individual at several levels: nationally, where stable political structures are important; in employment, where uncertainty results in lower output; and as a person, where anxiety prevents a person from performing effectively. As soon as these needs are satisfied, the next set emerges:

BELONGINGNESS AND LOVE NEEDS

The group 'belongingness' reflects humankind's social nature. Isolation and ostracism have a negative impact on the well-being of a person. The group 'love needs' is about giving and receiving affection – a mutuality of exchange, stresses Maslow. The next step in the hierarchy he calls:

ESTEEM NEEDS

Maslow divides these needs into two parts. The first is to do with achievement, adequacy and competence, what he saw as the need for self-esteem. The other is the esteem of others in being recognized as a person of dignity, value and, for some, reputation and prestige. The ultimate set of needs he describes as:

SELF-ACTUALIZATION

'What humans can be, they must be,' writes Maslow. 'They must be true to their own nature.'[12] Such needs vary enormously from person to person; in contrast, for example, with the universal physiological needs, they are powerful motivators because they allow people to discover their true potential.

Maslow's theory has had a powerful impact on psychology as well as on counselling and psychotherapy. He is seen as one of the founders of humanistic psychology, the so-called Third Psychology, in contrast to psychoanalytic and behaviourist psychology.

Humanistic psychology and its offspring, humanistic counselling, count among their adherents the person-centred approach of Carl Rogers, the 'transactional analysis' popularized by Eric Berne, and the Gestalt Movement associated with the name of Fritz Perls. It includes many others who share a common view of our human nature which can be summarized as follows:

Every human being is unique and has intrinsic worth.

Human nature is holistic; that is, the physical, the emotional and the spiritual are inseparable.

People are basically social and can only develop and grow in relationship with others.

People are capable of choice.

Self-esteem is a basic human need.

People are basically good with the potential and resources to live effectively.

Some Christians are attracted to the humanistic psychological approaches of Maslow, for many of the characteristics listed above are wholly biblical. Yet it has two major shortcomings. The first is the emphasis on the 'basically good' aspect of human nature. The humanistic school denies the results of the Fall – that men and women need redemption through Christ.

The second is the emphasis on the self apart from God.[11] Maslow recognizes this shortcoming in his later writings. His Third Psychology was then perceived as:

transitional, a preparation for a still higher fourth psychology,
transpersonal, transhuman, centred in the cosmos rather than in human
needs and interest, going beyond humanness, identity, self-actualiza-
tion and the like.[14]

For the Christian, this 'fourth psychology' is already present, with
Maslow's cosmos substituted by its creator. Compared with his
influence in psychology, therapy and counselling, Maslow has had less
impact in business. His hierarchy of needs is often presented at training programmes but defies simple, practical application. It is another
writer from a similar tradition to Maslow who has had a much greater
impact in the business world. His views can be represented as:

Man in Tension

Frederick Herzberg

Frederick Herzberg was an international management celebrity of
the '60s and '70s. The reliability of his research, which led to his
original conclusions, has been severely criticized and he is now less
fashionable than he was. He has some interesting insights, however,
which are helpful in our exploration. Chief amongst these is the way
he bases his view of human nature on Old Testament exegesis, drawing on rabbinic traditions.

According to Herzberg, the Old Testament contains two significant versions of the nature of man. The first of these he calls Adamic,
based on the creation story; the second Abrahamic, based on the
covenant between God and Abraham. The Adam version asserts that
man was created without knowledge ('feeble-minded') yet was able
to enjoy the world in which he lived. Things changed when he ate of
the fruit of the tree of knowledge. That action prompted his expulsion from Eden and his being consigned to a life characterized by
suffering and pain. By way of contrast, the Abraham version demonstrates man's potential, a characteristic which is reinforced by God
choosing him to be his earthly representative.

Having introduced these two conflicting views, Herzberg argues that those in positions of power have variously used them to bolster their authority. Thus, Moses emphasized the Abrahamic (human potential) model as a means of building a society different from that of Egypt. With the introduction of kings, however, the emphasis switched to the importance of rules and regulations (Adamic) as a means of protecting the status quo. Such manipulation, asserts Herzberg, has continued in those countries with a Judaeo-Christian heritage and he cites the Middle Ages, the Renaissance and the Reformation to demonstrate his case. Developing his view further as a precursor to his research work on human motivation, he states categorically that the Industrial Revolution and Capitalism have conspired together, as it were, to reinforce the Adamic view at the cost of the Abrahamic, as a means of exercising control to their own benefit. It is against this background that Herzberg puts forward his theories of motivation.

His original research was conducted in Pittsburgh, Pennsylvania and based on an extensive programme of questionnaires and interviews which asked employees 'about events they had experienced at work which either had resulted in a marked improvement in their job satisfaction, or had led to a marked reduction in job satisfaction.'[15] The results, which were repeated over and over again in subsequent experiments, can be simply summarized.

Herzberg divides people's needs into two groupings. The first of these, which he calls hygiene factors, are the needs for good working relationships, for reasonable levels of pay and for intelligible and fair administrative policies and procedures. All of these have to be satisfied before people can be motivated. Their absence or distortion is the source of considerable dissatisfaction, but they do not, of themselves, become the source of satisfaction and hence the means of positive motivation. Positive motivators, asserts Herzberg, are of an entirely different kind. They include achievement, recognition, responsibility and work itself. In order to facilitate the motivation of others, work has to be designed in such a way that it enables people to fulfil their potential, to exercise control over what they are doing and to gain recognition for their achievements.

The success of Herzberg's work was partly due to his charismatic personality and partly to the practicability of his proposed solutions.

The phrase 'job enrichment' was coined to enable jobs to be restructured in such a way that people felt motivated by them. His ideas were widely espoused in business. Thirty years after his initial work, he is less widely quoted although many in management continue to use the phrase 'hygiene factors' flippantly but accurately. But the lasting influence of his work is still to be seen, particularly in the concept of empowerment which has achieved a powerful following in the '90s.

Herzberg's theory is rooted in the Judaeo-Christian tradition and resonates with the scriptures more than most. It falls short of the comprehensive biblical view on two grounds. First, it imposes a distinction between work and non-work which fails to honour the integration of the person and the world in which he or she exists. Second, it takes no account of the transcendent, the sense of the divine, which Maslow saw lacking in humanistic psychology and which can only be truly discovered through the transforming power of Christ's work.

Developing Man

The final approach to motivation, characterized by Ed Schein, is less well known than the others hitherto discussed. It is important, however, because it takes into account both the complexity of human nature and the diversity of human development.

Ed Schein

Ed Schein was Professor of Occupational Psychology at the Massachusetts Institute of Technology. He suggests that a realistic assessment of human motivation must take into account two important features:

HUMAN DIVERSITY

Human behaviour is unpredictable, argues Schein, for no two people are wholly alike. Those who watch soap operas will undoubtedly agree, finding it difficult to believe the behaviourists' claim that all people with a similar socio-economic background are likely to behave in the same way towards the same situation. So, too, will those who have worked in any organization that employs people with a similar educational background and similar professional qualifications to do similar work. They will also have observed difficult-to-explain differences between the behaviour of 'A' as compared with that of 'B'. Our own observations support Schein's conclusion that it is not possible to predict a group of behaviour regardless of the detail which is available about its background and task.

HUMAN DEVELOPMENT

The other important feature highlighted by Schein (and largely ignored elsewhere in the literature on motivation) is the pattern of human development, in particular, that of adult development. At different times of our life we are likely to be motivated by different aspects of work. Those in their 20s, for example, may well be motivated by acquiring qualifications and classifying the appropriate context in which to work. Ten years later the same people may be motivated, predominantly, by achievement. Later still, control of their environment may be the major factor, whereas in their 50s, security and consolidation may assume the greatest force.

Once again, we need the reminder that patterns are useful as generalizations, but that generalizations are dangerous; exceptions can immediately be found to counter any universal rule. Schein's views are introduced at this point as a bridge between the theories of his fellow management writers and the practical approach we need for pastoral care. His views reinforce the biblical teaching that each person is unique, growing and developing in his or her own way from helpless infancy to adult maturity. He advises managers – we can substitute pastoral carers at this point – to:

be good diagnosticians and value a spirit of enquiry

learn to value differences

be flexible enough and have the interpersonal skills necessary to vary their own behaviour.[16]

The Biblical Approach

In describing these theories of motivation and human nature, I have commented on how they measure up against the biblical view. Before we move on to strategies for pastoral care, let us summarize briefly what the Bible emphazises on this topic.

Human Predicament

The Bible portrays men and women as having disobeyed God and, therefore, no longer able to enjoy a fulfilling relationship with him, within themselves, with their fellow humans and with the created world in which they live. Enslaved by sin, they pursue that which is selfish, without regard to the consequences to others, to the wider community or to their environment. This pursuit, however, does not satisfy them and they experience alienation, frustration and despair. This biblical portrait needs no illustration or proof. It can be seen every day in the home, at work, at school, on the TV and in the newspapers. This is the human predicament.

Human Destiny

Set against that predicament is the destiny of humankind. Men and women still retain the image of God, even though it is distorted. They are valued and loved by God, whose son Jesus was born as a man so that through his death and resurrection, men and women could aspire to the full image, as represented by Jesus. So men and women, through God's common and special grace, have the potential to live life as it should be lived — at one with God.

Human Motivation

The Christian recognizes this human paradox in his or her everyday activities. For the Christian, the motivation to work is to honour and worship God who, from the very beginning, created men and women as workers like himself.

Strategies for Pastoral Care

How can we help those who have lost the desire to work? What can we say to those who find work utterly frustrating? And what of those for whom the prospect of getting to work each day seems an intolerable burden? We may not have encountered a character such as Tom, but most of us can point to examples of those who have lost the motivation they once had. We might even have fallen into such a state ourselves from time to time.

The summary of motivational themes we have just displayed reminds us of the dangers of generalizations. However sound the theory may seem, it is always possible to find an exception or two which demonstrate that it is a theory and not a law. Those in positions of responsibility in employment work – be they in business, education, government, health, etc. – have to generalize in order to make policies. Pay systems and career development programmes have to be based on a concept of human behaviour if they are going to be effective. The fact that many of them are not effective is because the basic assumptions about people are usually wrong.

But those engaged in pastoral care are usually face-to-face with a person. It is the person who has the problem and needs our help and support. From what we have learned in the earlier part of this chapter and from the biblical view of work set out in chapter two, here are a number of interdependent strategies that can be tailored to meet the needs of the people you are seeking to help:

Understanding the Person

Listen to their Story

The starting point is to listen and allow the person to tell his or her story. Do not focus on the presenting problem, for you will only learn about the problem and not the person. Demonstrate that you have listened by summarizing from time to time and reflecting on particular points. Spot the themes which recur and note the connections they make.

Note their Development

As they tell their story, note their stage of personal development. There are many models which can be used to help. Erik Erikson's epigenetic matrix is a practical tool despite its extraordinary title.[17] Frank Lake's 'Chair of Identity'[18] is another model which is specifically Christian; so, too, is James Fowler's;[19] he uses the work of Erikson and others for his model of faith development. The importance of these models is to aid understanding: understanding both *of* and *by* the individual. For someone like Tom to discover that his loss of desire to achieve is very common among people of his age, can be of comfort. To learn that it marks the beginning of another stage of the journey and is not a sign of senile decay can be enormously liberating. Use these frameworks but beware that they do not become straitjackets. There are general stages of development but God has made us all unique.

Provide another Perspective

Seeing ourself through someone else's eyes can be a valuable experience. To do this, some sort of instrument is required which can be communicated easily to the other person. Many of these instruments exist and are frequently based on theories of personality.

These instruments are often referred to as personality tests and are of two sorts. The first are called 'normative tests' and can be used to compare one person with another. A good example is Cattell's '16 PF'[20] which provides a profile against 16 carefully defined personality traits. The second sort are called 'ipsative tests', which provide information about the comparative strength or weakness of specific characteristics, but do not compare individuals with any others. An example which is widely used in business and Christian circles is the Myers Briggs Type Inventory.[21] Based on Jung's theory of personality, the person is scored against four dimensions: extraversion–introversion; sensing–intuition; thinking–feeling; controlled–spontaneous. The combination of these scores is assembled to form a person's type.[22]

These tests can be valuable aids but can only be interpreted by an authorized person. Pastoral counsellors do not have to use them and can develop their own instruments to help the person who has turned to them for help, to 'see themselves as others see them'.

Clarifying their Situation

In the course of telling their story, you will have heard of the difficulties your clients are encountering; specifically, their loss of motivation for work. Sometimes, the causes will be obvious but normally they are not – at least, not to the person who has come to see you. You can provide support by helping them to clarify their situation. To do this, you should collect together information about a number of features:

The Nature of the Task Itself
Get them to describe what they do. Has their work a purpose which can be clearly defined? Does it make demands on their skills and abilities? How does it fit into the overall work of the section or department?

The Social Contacts Involved
Is the task achieved by a team or by the individual? What contact is there with colleagues, with suppliers and with customers?

The Culture of the Organization
Culture has been defined as 'the way we do things here'. It is the atmosphere and ethos of the place. Is their work culture formal or

informal? trusting or cynical? excellence or anything goes?

From these descriptions, and using the material summarized earlier in the chapter, it should be possible to decide on the prevailing view on human nature taken by the company, and the management style adopted to motivate other people. It will not be possible to change it (unless the person is, like Tom, at the head of the organization), but clarification can set the scene for the major aspect of pastoral care which can be offered to clients, and which is described as follows:

Finding God in All Things

These words form the title of a book by Margaret Hebblethwaite[23] which is an introduction to the Spiritual Exercises of St Ignatius. There is a short paragraph which is pertinent to the topic we are exploring. She writes:

> *We can find God by exploring to the ends of the earth, but we can also find God when confined to a narrow prison. We can find God by becoming a mother, or we can find God by becoming a nun. We can find God by reading a holy book, or we can find God by reading the newspaper. It depends rather on whether we are looking for God, than on whether we have the right opportunities. We can find God in all things.[24]*

And we can find God in our place of work, even though what we are doing may fail to satisfy, to fulfil or to motivate us. Indeed the phrase 'even though' might be substituted by 'particularly when', for when our need is greatest, God is already there. We saw in an earlier chapter that God's work is – at various times – creative, sustaining and redemptive. We saw, too, that human work resembles that of God, for we were made in his image and are co-workers with him. Those in a pastoral role can use this three-fold nature of work to help others to find God in all things.

Acknowledging his Lordship

Whatever you do, work at it with all your heart, as working for the Lord, not for man. (Colossians 3:23)

Paul wrote these words for slaves. They had no rights as they were the property of their owners. They had to undertake the most unpleasant duties, for such was their prescribed lot in life. They received little or no reward save that of basic subsistence. Yet, writes Paul, even in dire straits such as these we can find God and, what is more, we can acknowledge his lordship. 'The task may appear unimportant,' comments Nicholas Wright, 'but the person doing it is never that, and he or she has the opportunity to turn the job into an act of worship.'[25]

5

WORK: CHOICE OR CALLING?

> *Each one should remain in the situation which he was in*
> *when God called him.*
>
> (1 Corinthians 7:20)

We now turn our attention to Nick. His story will lead us into a discussion of vocation, a significant topic for Christians in the context of work, yet one which is frequently misunderstood.

Nick's Story

Nick is in his mid-20s. He became a Christian in his late teens and has played an active part in his home church, as well as in the Christian Union whilst at university. Nick's parents attend church very infrequently and only for major festivals. His mother is a local magistrate, his father a senior partner in a financial services firm in the City of London. He has an elder brother who is a solicitor and doing extremely well.

Like his brother, Nick was sent to an independent school as a dayboy. His father was very ambitious for both of them and, for a while, was very concerned lest Nick's faith led to his 'doing something stupid with his life'. He had dissuaded Nick from taking a gap year between school and university, feeling that he might lose the motivation to study.

Nick graduated in English with a good degree. In his final year at university he was very unclear as to what he should do. He had applied to a number of voluntary agencies but soon discovered they were more interested in water engineers or nurses than in those who had specialized in the novels of Virginia Woolf. He had also given some thought to teaching and to social work, but decided against either of them after his father learned of the possibility and read the riot act to him.

Nick attended the university milk round and was offered a job by his present employer. He was particularly influenced in his choice by the interviewer, who had worn a silver fish symbol in his coat lapel.

His father and his elder brother had encouraged him strongly to accept the position. Peter, the vicar of his home church, had said nothing but Nick sensed his disappointment. Some of his friends from the Christian Union had challenged him as to whether he could reconcile his faith with the sort of work and lifestyle he would have to adopt. Nick took refuge in the lapel badge and accepted the offer.

He has been with the organization now for 18 months. Work is conducted in a highly charged, competitive atmosphere. Nick is doing well and more than holding his own. He wishes there were more person-to-person contact and less reliance on technology for communication but that is a minor concern. His major concern arises from two aspects of the job. The first is that he is expected to work very long hours. This he does, but he is finding that he can give less and less time to church activities. The regularity of his prayer time and Bible reading is also suffering. The second concern is that he is becoming more and more dependent on his very high salary. Both concerns are making him wonder whether he was right to have chosen the job in the first place. Should he have stood up to his father and pursued

a teaching career? How can he discover what is God's will
for him?

The Christian's Calling

Nick is in a privileged position. Many people of his age are unemployed with little hope of getting a worthwhile occupation. Theirs is
a different problem which is not addressed here. Nick, however, is far
from unique – many young Christians ask themselves whether they
are in the right job. They may have joined a particular employer for
what seemed the right reason at the time but now are having second
thoughts. Alternatively, they may find that the job is giving them little
or no satisfaction at all, and they want to move to something else
which might.

But the issue is not only about choosing a job at an early age like
Nick. Christians of all ages have to make choices about work at various times of their life. Christine, the curate's wife, who was present
at that earlier meeting, is one such example.

Christine's predicament will serve to introduce another work-
related issue in chapter seven, but her situation is not uncommon.
When a man offers himself for ordination, the impact on his wife can
be substantial. It might mean that she has to leave her job and move
elsewhere, either or both of which can lead to tensions in the
marriage. Similar tensions may arise when it is the woman being
ordained or when new employment is offered to one member of a
career couple. Until a few years ago, it was nearly always the male's
career that took precedence over the female's. That scenario is
rapidly changing with a wife's career becoming equally important to
that of her husband.

How do Christians face up to these matters? How do they discover
the right work for themselves? Where does the concept of vocation
come into the equation? And what sort of pastoral care can you offer
to them?

Vocation

In dealing with these questions, we will consider first the concept of vocation. It is a concept which, in the opinion of Dietrich Bonhoeffer, is 'of almost unique significance for the history of ethics'.[1] It certainly is a fundamental one for Christians in their work.

Vocation in the Secular Sense

The word 'vocation' has entered into common usage in the sense of a job or career. Vocational guidance is given to young people at school, whereby teachers or career advisers help them identify the sort of work that might be suitable. This sometimes leads to a course of study, or provides the platform from which the young person can make an appropriate move into the world of employment work.

Vocational qualifications have been devised to measure a person's progress in a chosen field of endeavour. The competence to perform specific tasks is assessed by observing people's behaviour and examining their theoretical knowledge. Achievement is recognized by certification.

A further variation of the secular use of the word is the notion of vocational occupations. Nurses are a good case in point here and so are teachers. Shopkeepers and accountants are not. Implicit in this use of the word is a sense of service allied to the intrinsic value of the work itself. Many of these vocational occupations are jobs traditionally done by women, usually low-paid but held in high regard by others. This raises some interesting questions about 'women's work' which we will answer when we turn our attention to Sally in chapter nine.

For the time being, let us note that all three secular uses of the word 'vocation' make it synonymous with work, occupation or career.

Vocation in the Christian Sense

The fundamental difference between the idea of vocation described above and that of Christian vocation is that the latter involves God. The word 'vocation' comes from the Latin 'vocare' which simply means to call. For the Christian, vocation presupposes that there is someone who calls and that someone is God. Among Christians, there exist three popular misconceptions of the word:

Christians are Called to a Particular Occupation

This suggests that each of us has a specific occupation to which we are called by God, and through which we live out our calling as Christians. This view is associated with Luther, who was keen to combat the exclusive claims of monastic or clerical calling. Luther took a strong line on this subject (as he did on many others!), insisting from 1 Corinthians 7:20 that each of us has a specific place in life. His emphasis was a necessary one to make in order to combat the prevailing views. It was, though, a distorted one, criticized by Bonhoeffer – himself a Lutheran – as 'pseudo-Lutheranism'.[2] This distortion limits the idea of calling to secular work and, in Bonhoeffer's opinion, suggests that Christians should always accept the social status quo. The verse from Mrs Alexander's hymn, now deleted from many contemporary hymnbooks, encapsulates this misconception of calling:

> *The rich man in his castle.*
> *The poor man at his gate,*
> *God made them poor and mighty*
> *and ordered their estate.*

Christians are Called to a Particular State

This second notion is the one which was attacked by Luther. It claims that there are certain states to which Christians can aspire, the highest of which is the contemplative life. (This represented the supreme call of God, embodied in the monastic tradition of separateness from the world.) It suggests a division between a life of prayer and a life of work which is not substantiated anywhere in scripture and is, as we saw in chapter two, contrary to the teaching of scripture. Mary, the sister of Lazarus, is identified as the patron saint of the contemplatives, with Martha representing the workers who engage in the lower state of active service. Interestingly enough, this distinction is roundly opposed by one of the great 'contemplatives', St Teresa of Avila. Writing of Martha, she comments:

> *If contemplation and mental and vocal prayer and tending the sick and serving in the house and working at even the lowliest tasks are of service to the guest (Jesus) who comes to stay with us and to eat and take his recreation with us, what should it matter to us if we do one of these things rather than another?*[3]

A variation on this theme is the vocation to celibacy. This provokes debate in the Roman Catholic Church because of its link with the priesthood. It provokes a different sort of debate among evangelicals because of its link with marriage and divorce.[4] It is mentioned here because it serves as a bridge between the call to a particular state and to the next misconception:

Christians are Called to Ordained Ministry
This equates calling with the specific role of the ordained clergy. It suggests an inner call by God which is experienced by the individual. That such an inner call happens is well substantiated both in scripture and in personal experience. Christopher Bryant, who uses the phrase 'inner compulsion' to describe the call, instances Jeremiah, Amos, Paul and William Wilberforce to reinforce the point.[5] It is supported by the Ordinal of the Church of England where the bishop asks:

> *Do you believe, so far as you know your own heart, that God has called you to be to the office and work of a deacon/priest in his church?*[6]

This misconception is that such an inner sense of calling is exclusively to ordained ministry, the notion of which is, as Francis Dewar points out, 'relatively recent in the history of the Church.'[7] It cannot be denied, but it needs to be understood in a wider biblical context to which we will now turn.

The Biblical View of Vocation

Our Vocation Comes from God

The distinction between the secular and the Christian use of the word vocation is that the latter presupposes someone who calls. That is our starting point which is well attested in scripture; both Old and New Testaments are full of references to God's calling. In the Old Testament, the most frequent use occurs in Isaiah, especially chapter 40 onwards (for example, 41:9; 43:1; 48:1, etc.). In the New Testament, Paul refers to it most often (for example, Romans 1:6; 8:28; 1 Corinthians 1:24; Galatians 5:3, etc.), with Peter and the writer to the Hebrews also doing so (for example, 1 Peter 1:15; Hebrews 9:15, etc.).

God Calls Us as a Community

God calls Israel to be his people. His calling addresses them as a corporate entity. The calling originates in his gracious love and is realized in the covenant. This is made abundantly clear in Isaiah where God proclaims that, despite the people's frequent failures, he remains steadfast. 'The hand of God initiates [the call],' comments Alec Motyer on Isaiah 48:13, 'and the call of God sovereignly dictates the outcome.'[8]

The New Testament makes the same emphasis, a point highlighted and developed in Steve Walton's book on vocation.[9] One important example of this is the Greek word for church, 'ekklesia', which has, as its root, the word for 'call'. Christians are called to a corporate life, to become the Church. The individualism with which we are so familiar in the Western Church is a far cry from the corporate emphasis in the New Testament. All the metaphors for the Church such as body, nation, or priesthood are collective ones. We are called as a community to a corporate life.

God Calls Us as Individuals

God called Samuel (1 Samuel 3:4, 6, 8); he called Paul (Romans 1:1; 1 Corinthians 1:1, etc.); and he called many others as individuals. In all cases they were called for a specific purpose, a feature of the biblical view of calling which we shall consider shortly. First, though, we need to see the purpose of God's calling.

God Calls Us to be Holy

Israel is called by God to be the holy people (Exodus 22:1; Isaiah 62:12), reflecting the holiness of the One who has called them (Leviticus 19:2). So, too, Christians are called to be holy (Romans 1:7 – the word translated 'saints' can also be translated 'holy'), reflecting the holiness of Jesus (1 Peter 1:15). This calling is to belong wholly to Jesus, writes Dietrich Bonhoeffer:

> [It] embraces work with things and relationships with persons; it demands a 'limited field of accomplishments', yet never as a value in itself, but in responsibility towards Jesus Christ. [10]

Holiness in the scriptures has two aspects. The first is that of being set apart, consecrated to the service of God. The second is that of moral uprightness. Both of these aspects are to characterize our lifestyle. It is the purpose of our calling and it affects the whole of our life.

God's Calling Embraces Work

Steve Walton uses the metaphor of a building to describe the biblical view of vocation. [11] The call to belong to Jesus Christ is, he suggests, the foundation. The call to holiness and a corporate life represents the ground floor. The next level up is the call to give God first place in our life. It is only when these structures are in place that we move to the top storey and consider the particular roles or tasks that God would have us do. It follows that any task we undertake or role we perform is an aspect of our calling. For Paul, it was to be an apostle (Romans 1:1). For each of us it will be something different; perhaps a parent, a housewife, a bricklayer, a bus driver or an architect.

Moreover, it can change from time to time because the calling is for the whole of our lives and not that part of it represented by the roles we discharge. At one time we may be called to work in an office, at another in the home, at yet another as an ordained minister. God's call is to each and every one of us, in whatever situation we find ourselves and to whatever position we aspire. This is particularly well captured by the bestselling author, the psychiatrist M. Scott Peck. Telling his story as a Christian, he explains his calling to be an author. Writing books, he observes, 'may be my own "grand vocation" [but] I believe I previously did have a genuine calling to psychiatry and to government service.'[12]

Making Choices as Christians

Let us now return to Nick and look at some of the environmental features influencing his choice of work. As we do this, I will make reference to several of the other characters from the meeting. The following four typical situations should be borne in mind:

1. **Starting work**. The focus here is on teenagers and young adults, with Nick's situation representing such a group.

2. **Changing voluntarily**. This may be to another organization or to something completely different. Christine's husband, James, moved from business to theological college and then to parochial ministry. Retirement might also feature here, although more attention will be given to that in a later chapter.

3. **Relocation**. One marriage partner moving to another part of the country impacts on the other and on their family. Christine has had to change her job because of James' choice.

4. **Starting a family**. Sally represents thousands of married women who, on starting a family, are faced with the choice of returning after maternity leave or devoting their time and energies to their children and other unpaid work.

Factors Influencing our Choice of Work

Availability of Work
The idea of choice of work presupposes the availability of work. This is an unreal presupposition for many in countries where high unemployment is a feature of contemporary society. I believe that, as Christians, we must struggle with this evil, this further dehumanization of God's creatures made in his image. Unemployment is not, however, the subject matter of this book which, as far as this chapter is concerned, is about helping those who wish to make choices. I shall assume, therefore, that those who come to us for help in this context, do so with the opportunity of choice as a practical reality.

Financial Circumstances
Even if money is not the main factor for some, it certainly is a major one for most. Nick and Tom, in this respect, are the exceptions. Nick, for example, has no dependents and few financial commitments. Any choice which he makes impacts on him alone. Tom has become financially independent and could stop work without too much difficulty. Monica, on the other hand, has no choice. She is the breadwinner and it looks as if she will remain so. People in Frank's position prior to early retirement have little choice too, for, with their long service, a premature departure severely damages their pension entitlement.

Location
The geographical place of work may be important, particularly for those whose children are at school, who have ageing parents to support or who do not wish to sever their connections with a local church.

Capability and Competence
It often seems that other people's jobs are much easier than our own. We could all make sounder political and economic judgements than the Prime Minister, or run the public transport system better than

the Chief Executive Officer, or be a more effective minister than the one we currently have at the church where we worship. Yet if we ever seek to change what we are doing to do something else, we discover that others view our competence differently. Except, of course, in the case of parenthood, for which no training or prior skill is required!

Despite his academic qualifications, Nick could not get a place with an aid agency because he did not have the necessary skills. Frank would have difficulty finding paid employment at a level of income matching that which he received at the bank, because his abilities would not be valued in the same way by another employer. Contemporary writers like William Bridges,[13] Charles Handy[14] and Peter Herriot[15] urge us to develop multiple skills which can be transferred from one environment to another. There is much wisdom in their exhortation but it is not easy for some to follow their advice, particularly those, like Monica and her husband Alf, who have had few opportunities for education or skill-training early in their lives.

Family

Parental influence may be in the form of pressure, as in the case of Nick's father. Many young people are attracted to particular occupations because they wish to follow in the footsteps of their mother or father. This can give great satisfaction to all concerned but it sometimes results in conflict; for example, when the son or daughter makes a mess of the family business.

Partners may also influence job choice. The young adults who have lived a fairly carefree existence before marriage, may decide to 'settle down' when they marry, which involves them choosing different sorts of occupation. And then there are those who want their partners to behave in a particular way: the ambitious wife who wants her husband to succeed; the ambitious man who wants his wife to support him; the Christian – and for that matter the non-Christian – who believes that the woman's place is in the home amongst the family.

The major influence of children is felt on the economic front. It is felt before the first child is born and can continue into young adulthood and well beyond.

Friends

For the young it is often an older person who is a major source of influence: the caring careers adviser at school; the youth leader; an adult who becomes a role model. Later, it may be a contemporary whose influence will chiefly be that of support, but occasionally that of advice and guidance.

Faith

What is my mission in life? This question neatly encapsulates the many aspects of the interdependence of living and working. It is a question that comes at the very end of Richard Bolles' bestselling annual *What Color is your Parachute?*.[16] In the late '60s, Bolles (an American clergyman) noted with concern how many of the Christians to whom he ministered found their work wearisome and untouched by their faith. He began to put together notes to help them in their choice of work and discovered that he was meeting a massive need from within and outside the Christian Church. In 1970 he published the first edition of what has become an annual publication. A quarter of a century later it has sold over five million copies and is the best do-it-yourself guide to those engaged in career change and job hunting.

Despite its success outside the Christian community, Bolles has never forgotten the original purpose of the book and concludes his book each year with the question: What is my mission in life? He starts from the premise that faith and work should not be compartmentalized and stresses that the question is not a problem to be solved but a journey to be undertaken. He suggests three parts of everyone's mission which can be generalized as follows:

To be conscious of God in whatever we do or wherever we work.

Under the influence of the Holy Spirit, to strive to make the place in which we work a better place.

To use our God-given talents in our place of work so as to achieve God's purposes.[17]

A mission such as this fits well with the biblical view of work we encountered in chapter two. Having recognized that all these factors influence our work choice, let us now consider how we can best provide appropriate pastoral care.

Strategies for Pastoral Care

Summarized below are four stages which you can use in your ministry of pastoral care with individuals facing choices about work. Further suggestions on pastoral care for groups are made in chapter ten.

Get to Know the Person

The first two points under this heading are similar to those in the previous chapter on motivation. I suggest that you refer to the comments made there on understanding personality and the person's development. A few additional comments on the topics are made here.

Recognize and Affirm their Personality

Many are helped when another person reflects back to them aspects of themselves they may not have considered before. They are given a new framework, a new perspective whereby they can see themselves in a different light. Such insight can be a powerful aid when choosing work, for it may suggest avenues previously ignored. Some jobs are more suited to people of a particular disposition or temperament than others. This is well documented in career guidance manuals although care must be taken in the use of such links, for there is not much evidence of positive correlation between distinct personality profiles and success in specific tasks. Treat the profiles as general directions and not as detailed guides, but do use them – they can be of great value.

Appreciate their State of Development

Shakespeare's seven ages of man reminds us that men and women may function best when their work complements their personal development. This is a much neglected area in the design of work. Indeed, the expectation in many organizations today is that people should be capable of performing at a certain level regardless of their age or state of development. There are signs, however, that some employers are recognizing that both energy and wisdom are required for success and that they come in different ratios with age.

Acknowledge their Personal Circumstances

Finding the right position which fits a person's temperament and personal development will engender great satisfaction, but it may not pay the bills. In providing pastoral care, you need to know a sufficient amount about the personal circumstances of the person you are supporting. Failure to do so can have painful consequences, as is illustrated in the case of Christine and her husband, James, the curate. It is all too easy to overlook personal circumstances, especially financial ones, because it appears to be prying.

What is more, many Christians are unwilling to be honest about their financial state, not least because it seems to be rather lacking in faith. Did not Jesus himself commend practices which sacrificed family and personal relationships (Luke 14:25–27)? Yet we would do well to recall that in the parables following Jesus' call to discipleship, he urged the necessity of forethought (Luke 14:28–33). Moreover, he never called on us to renounce our responsibilities or our duties to those dependent on us.

Understand their Competence

Anyone involved in education or employment will know that the word 'competence' has assumed a new importance in the '80s and '90s. The meaning attributed to it has become more precise and the word is now used to represent the way a person combines their skill, knowledge and experience to perform specific tasks. The competence of students at school and university, and employees in countless organizations, is assessed as their performance of discrete tasks is observed and evaluated. Achievement is rewarded and promotions are made on the basis of successful performance. In providing pastoral care in this area, three competence issues are important:

Realism

When Nick applied for a position with an aid agency, he had to face the reality that he lacked the necessary competence. This would have been an easy message for the agency to convey, and we can assume that Nick accepted it. But not all of those you deal with accept the realities so readily. Frank might be such a person. Helping people to take stock of their strengths and limitations is a vital ingredient of successful pastoral care in this area. Encourage them to tell you – or to write down – their particular strengths and to describe to you the evidence for their claims. People often overestimate or underestimate their competence. You can help them to be realistic.

Opportunity

Another jargon phrase much in vogue at present is that of 'transferable skills'. This simply means that the competence developed in one set of circumstances (for example at school or in employment) can be transferred to another, different set of circumstances.

This is a liberating concept if it can be applied, for it suggests that someone is not restricted to one line of occupation, but can switch between occupations. It is not about moving between businesses but doing similar work, as has been the case in many trades and professions. It means taking a particular competence, for example, negotiating skills or high-level manual dexterity, and transferring it to something entirely different.

As you exercise your pastoral care, you can help those you serve to discover new opportunities for the use of their competence. Monica's husband, Alf, seems intent on staying in one occupation, yet the skills and knowledge he has developed over the years might be capable of being used in a different context. You are unlikely to have

the knowledge yourself to identify the range of occupations for someone like Alf, but you can encourage him to break out from his narrow
self-limiting view to a much broader one.

Gifts

For much of this century, evangelical Christians have given
prominence to certain gifts, particularly those associated with
preaching and teaching. In some ways, there are parallels in Western
society which has accorded much greater value to linguistic, logical
and conceptual skills than it has done to others. The charismatic
movement has enabled us to recognize anew the diversity of God's
gifts. It has enriched our communal Christian life and given a
great deal of self-esteem to some Christians who previously felt
undervalued.

The call to recognize and develop people's talents is beginning to
infiltrate education and business circles through concepts such as
those contained in Howard Gardner's work.[18] Gardner, who is a
Professor of Education at Harvard University, postulates that there
are seven distinct 'intelligences' rather than one. These seven he
names as linguistic, musical, logical–mathematical, spatial, bodily–
kinesthetic, inter-personal and intra-personal. He suggests that
formal education supports few of these and argues for a more creative
approach to the recognition and development of the gifts of each
person. His work has similarities to the views of the radical Christian
writers of the '60s, Ivan Illich[19] and Paolo Freire,[20] who saw education
in Western societies as a socialization process designed to maintain
the status quo. They supported moves towards the potential liberation which comes from recognizing the multi-faceted nature of
people's varied gifts.

In your pastoral caring role, your ability to recognize and encourage the use of each person's gifts in their occupation is a vital one.

Recognize Important Influences

Parents

Nick's father had a significant impact on his son's choice of job. In a very different way, Monica and Alf may have influenced their son who, as we shall learn later, has no employment at present. Parental influence takes so many forms. It may be of the direct sort as in Nick's case, or it may be much more supportive, recognizing the individual's own preference. It may be noticeable by its presence, as when a parent takes an active part in facilitating the choice, or it may be noted by its absence, when the young person is left to his or her own devices. Some children will be attracted to an occupation because of their parents' example, others will be repelled for the same reason. Sensitivity is required of you in gauging the extent of parental influence and of deciding whether it is to be supported or to be resisted.

Family and Friends

Similar sensitivity is required in respect of these groups. Expectations on the part of family and peer pressure from friends can have an influence on people which is difficult to resist at any age. You need to exercise wisdom in discerning whether that influence is for good or ill.

The Church

We have seen in this and earlier chapters some of the distorted teaching about work and calling. Some of you may be able to redress that teaching in a corporate context through influencing the content of sermons and study guides on the subjects. You can certainly enable the person you are helping to develop a new framework if the thinking has been conditioned by the sort of sacred/secular divide which lies at the root of many work-related problems. Seeing themselves through other eyes and seeing the world as God's world can open up a new dimension for all people and, at the same time, can be life-giving and liberating.

Help to Define a Mission

We noted earlier the three-part breakdown suggested by Richard Bolles on the subject of finding our mission in life. Under each of these headings are some suggestions which you might wish to use.

Awareness of God

Enabling another person to recognize God's presence is a major contribution which can be made by you in your ministry of pastoral care. You may call it spiritual direction or pastoral counselling, or you may prefer Leanne Payne's description, 'Practising the Presence'[21] – it does not really matter. It means helping to change the person's perspective, to enable him or her to develop a different map of the world. A story from my own experience will serve as an illustration.

On starting work at Ford Motor Company many years ago, I was encouraged by my church leaders to view my place of work as a mission field. I did this assiduously, using lunch and tea breaks as opportunities for telling others about Christ. Yet I found the responsibility burdensome, a feeling I communicated one day to another Christian I had met in one of the repair shops. He asked me what it was that I felt so hard to carry. 'The responsibility of bringing Christ to this factory every day,' I replied. He paused for a moment. 'Do you not think Christ might be here already?' His reply enabled me to see both myself and God from a different perspective. God was in that place and I knew it not.

In your pastoral role, you can help people to discern God in the factory, the office, the shop, the school, the home. He is in all those places but we often do not know how to look.

Influenced by the Spirit

Bolles makes a connection between following the Holy Spirit's guidance and making the world a better place. This is a positive, biblical view even though the effect may, from time to time, be a painful one. We can view this in three distinct ways:

INSPIRING OUR ACTIVITIES

Bezalel is the first person in the Bible who is described by God as being filled with the Spirit (Exodus 31:2, 3). The Holy Spirit inspires us in our work to accomplish God's work. That may sound very grand, and applicable only to those whose work can in some way or other qualify as inspirational. Listen to the experience of Andrew Stokes who, as an industrial chaplain in Sheffield, used to visit a run-down engineering factory in that city.

> *The machine tools were old, the foreman disillusioned, the atmosphere dark and oily. The handful of men who worked there were on seven-day working: they worked, that is to say, every day of their lives except when the works shut down. They were sour, ill-tempered and unhappy. There was a labourer, called George, who made the tea and pushed round the floor a black thing which had once been a brush, and who completed the scene by having a hunch back and crossed eyes. I hated visiting this Dickensian nightmare, and so used to go on a Monday morning to get it over and done with. One such Monday in dirty mid-winter, I remember giving George a slap on his little hunch back and exclaiming mockingly, 'Well, George, and how are you enjoying your job this fine morning?' George looked up at me out of his crossed eyes and said 'Do you know, Vicar, I love my job. Just think what this place would get like if I didn't keep it clean for them.' I felt the shame which the centurion felt before the cross.*[22]

SHARING IN CHRIST'S SUFFERINGS

Mention of the cross brings us to the second aspect of 'making the world a better place'. This is achieved by joining with Christ in his redemptive work and sharing with him in his sufferings. Many places of work are devoted to questionable outputs, whose practices pay little attention to the divinity in man. They are characterized by exploitation, breeding in those who work in them attitudes of mistrust and cynicism. It is into such places that the Christian may choose to go as his or her mission in life. Another person in Andrew Stokes' book testifies to this:

> *We were like pigs at the trough. By contrast, for me, work had a three-*
> *fold divine purpose: to grow in the knowledge and love of God by work-*
> *ing and suffering with him; to serve my neighbour; and to free me from*
> *being self-centred by working with others for an objective other than*
> *my own. This approach could not have been more different from the*
> *prevailing view in which I worked. The Crucifixion never seemed more*
> *real to me than it did on Good Friday 1941, when I was working at a*
> *fitter's bench. I had a profound sense of being alone in an alien world.*
> *'My God, my God, why hast thou forsaken me?'*[23]

PROCLAIMING JUSTICE

The Holy Spirit may require us to execute a prophetic role in our place of work. The structures which evinced the responses reproduced from Andrew Stokes' book should not be accepted without question. I share Christian Schumacher's view that much work in developed countries is deformed work.[24] I also support William Temple's conclusion that 'a perfect saint [might be able] to perform the most wearisome and monotonous task "as unto God" [but] to ask any ordinary man so to regard monotonous drudgery ... is sheer mockery.'[25]

Our task, therefore, might be that of challenging the structures. This may be from a position of influence, such as Tom could exercise in his company. More often it is from a position of subordination in the hierarchy where criticism can easily result in ostracism or dismissal. Sometimes it is from a collective position, sharing with others in the combined struggle to reform and improve. The prophetic role is frequently a painful one. As someone engaged in pastoral care you may have to take sides and encourage the person to do so also. But do not desert them for they will need your help and support.

Using God's Gifts

Whether we use the biblical word 'talent', adopt the contemporary usage of 'competence' or employ Howard Gardner's 'multiple intelligences', the point is the same. God has given us abundant gifts, through the exercise of which we can glorify and worship him, serve others and grow towards the fullness of Christ as human beings created in God's image.

Through prayerful exploration, you can help the individual in your care to discern those gifts and, having done so, to begin to see where and how they can best be exercised. Some of Monica's gifts are certainly being used in the Guide movement and she may be using others in the chemical company. Nick is questioning whether he is in the best place to exercise his gifts and Sally, undoubtedly, needs some sort of assistance to help her see how she can make the most of what God has given to her.

Practical Guidance

Having done all these things, then, how can you go about the practical task of pointing people towards the most suitable occupation?

The answer to this question is, for the most part, to refer them elsewhere. Let us touch, briefly, on the resources available before we close the chapter with a look at decision making.

Career Counsellors

There are many people who offer expert guidance on job choice. These include the career guidance service provided in schools, colleges, universities and through government agencies. There are also private bodies whose quality varies from the outstanding to the mediocre. As a practical point, it is wise to collect together addresses and telephone numbers of these groups. There may, in addition, be people in your congregation who can help on this front, either because they are included among those who have the professional skills or because their experience seems to be suitable for providing appropriate help.

Self-Help

There are many such resources on the market and they range from the very detailed versions such as Richard Bolles' annual, to the quick-fix approach which suggests the whole process can be worked through in a matter of hours. Beware of the latter and use them as general guidelines rather than detailed workbooks.

Decision Making

Some people find decision making easy and others do not. Some do it quickly and others agonize for ages. Those who prefer a rational approach associate decision making with problem solving and set about it in a logical, step-by-step fashion. Others rely more on their intuition preferring the 'gut feel' to the reasoned conclusion.

There are no right and wrong ways of making decisions and each person will adopt what is most comfortable for them, or has worked for them in the past. For the Christian faced with choice, two partic-ular practices are commended which you can use at the beginning and end of each decision:

Commit it to God
The Collect for the nineteenth Sunday after Trinity (*Book of Common Prayer*) reads:

> *O God, forasmuch as without thee we are not able to please thee; Mercifully grant, that thy Holy Spirit may in all things direct and rule our hearts; through Jesus Christ our Lord. Amen.*

For the Christian, the starting point in any choice is that of pleasing God. Some of us forget this, making 'a means of the end and of the end a means so that, what they ought to seek first, they seek last.'[26] Encourage each person, therefore, to challenge their own priorities and thereby to discern whether the end (pleasing God) is more important than the means (a pleasing job).

Experience The Choices
Decisions are about choices; some people become concerned, having made the decision, that they have lost out by so doing. They become

aware of the benefits of the rejected choice when it is too late. This can easily lead to regrets which in turn undermine commitment to the path chosen. A helpful approach, adapted from St Ignatius' Spiritual Exercises,[27] is to experience the results of each choice in the imagination before it is made in reality. This can be of particular value where a job is concerned and when time is available. Encourage them, therefore, to spend a day or more living as though they had made a particular choice. During that time, they should give no thought to the alternative but reflect on their experience. At the end of the time allotted, they might share their experience with you or commit it to writing. Then they should adopt the same practice for the other choice over a similar period. For many people, the right choice becomes obvious and they can make their decision knowing that they have done so using all their faculties, and trusting that it has been taken for God's greater glory. Their work and God's work become one and the same thing.

6

STRESS AT WORK

When I was in distress, I sought the Lord.
(Psalm 77:2)

We turn now to the third participant in our church meeting: Monica, the Guide leader and chemical company employee.

Monica's Story

Monica married Alf almost 25 years ago. They are both 44 and live not far from the street where they grew up together. They have two children: Becky, who has one small child and another on the way, and Darren, who has never had a job since he left school three years ago. Darren is seldom seen by his parents any more for he has moved into a flat with a number of other young men and women. This is a great sadness to Monica although she is spared the thankless task of preventing him and his father from fighting – an activity which has become all too frequent in recent years.

When they were first married, Monica was involved with the Guides and Alf was a keen sportsman. Monica has retained her interest in the Guide movement throughout her married life and has been asked, on a number of occasions, to assume a prestigious role at county level. So far she has refused. Alf's only sporting activity now is that of the passive observer in front of the TV, although passive is a misleading adjective in that he is becoming ever more vociferous about the absence of skill among present-day soccer players, cricketers, athletes and the rest.

On leaving school, Alf served an apprenticeship as a millwright at a local engineering company. He worked there for the next 20 years enjoying the tradesman's privilege and higher rates of pay. He dismissed as the observations of the ignorant the comments of ex-colleagues that the company was failing to invest in new, sophisticated equipment. It was an enormous shock to him to learn on that fateful day five years ago that his employer was going into voluntary liquidation. After the shock had subsided, he felt quite euphoric as he received more than six months wages in redundancy pay and felt certain that he would pick up a new job in a matter of weeks. But it was not to be for, as his ex-colleagues had rightly predicted, Alf's skills applied to outdated machinery; he, like his insolvent employer, had never kept up to date. Five years later, he has given up any hope of getting a new job. He has taken part in several government training programmes but has made no secret of his determination that he will never demean himself to do work other than that which he describes as 'real men's work'. He hates being dependent on Monica and finds it increasingly difficult even to be polite to her. They spend little time in each other's company, their communication is at a minimum level, and they have not had a sexual relationship for at least two years.

Monica switched from part-time to full-time work four years ago, and is now employed in the packaging department of a medium-sized pharmaceutical firm. Prior to that, she had worked part-time for many years at a small supermarket. She had made the move in order to increase her earnings, for she had not shared Alf's optimism about his getting a new job and foresaw the need for a regular income. She explained her decision to Alf on the grounds that the extra money would enable Becky to have a really good wedding. The job she does is reasonable enough but her new supervisor is making enormous demands on her and her colleagues, which has removed a lot of the opportunity for socializing which has always meant so much to her. Now there is another problem: she has just been told by the head of the department that one of the big international pharmaceutical companies is rumoured to be making a bid for the firm.

Monica's problems are manifold. There is Alf's predicament, as well as Darren's. Their financial difficulties are on the increase and the situation at work has added further complications. She is sleeping badly and becoming increasingly irritable. Criticism of any sort reduces her to tears. She finds prayer very hard and seldom reads her Bible any more. Most things are a burden to her – even church and Guides. Monica is suffering from stress.

Stress

This chapter focuses on the topic of stress. It could almost be described as a fashionable topic, receiving an ever increasing amount of media attention. Many books have been written about it. Training programmes and self-help manuals on coping strategies are burgeoning. Stress counsellors are in great demand.

Stress is no respecter of persons: it affects both rich and poor; the employed and those out of work; men, women and children. Christians are not immune either, with ordained clergy and their spouses being particularly prone to it. It is costing industrial nations so much in healthcare and lost productivity that governments and employers are devoting substantial resources to its containment and prevention.

With Monica's situation firmly in our minds, we will address the causes of stress and consider some of the strategies which might be used to help her and the many others like her.

What is Stress?

An entry in Fowler's *A Dictionary of Modern English Usage* likens 'stress' and 'strain' to a 'pair of Siamese twins, suitably describing our worries and the effect they have on us'.[1] Fowler uses two words — 'stress' and 'strain' — but increasingly only the word 'stress' is used to describe the two different features encapsulated in that brief entry. Failure to make a distinction between these features frequently results in considerable misunderstanding.

A somewhat lengthier and very useful distinction will be adopted throughout this chapter. It comes from Rachel Jenkins,[2] who identifies the principal characteristics in contemporary common usage of the word. Used in one way, the word 'stress' describes the environmental demands which are imposed on us either by our personal circumstances, by ourselves or by those with whom we live and work. We often use 'pressure' as a synonym for this kind of stress and as such the word bears a neutral meaning. Most people can only function effectively if they are under a certain amount of stress of this sort; indeed, it is not unusual for people to create such stress in order to achieve whatever it is they have to do.

The other usage describes the psychological and physical symptoms which are the consequences of the environmental demands mentioned above. Used in this sense it has a negative connotation, for it suggests a misfit, a lack of congruence between individuals and their environment which seems to be beyond their capacity to control. Stress of this sort can result in mental illness of many different kinds including anxiety and depression. It may also result in physical illness or much more severe psychological conditions such as depressive psychosis and schizophrenia. The word 'distress' is sometimes used as a synonym for this sort of stress.

For the remainder of this chapter we will focus on this second meaning of stress, namely, the result of a mismatch between the person and his or her total environment.

The Origins and Effects of Stress

Writers on stress postulate that its origin stems from our innate reaction to threatening situations.[3] It is a viewpoint widely held. Thus, if we are faced with a seriously threatening situation we are likely to do one of two things. We might defend ourselves aggressively or we might run away, responses simply known as 'fight' or 'flight'. At such times, our bodies react spontaneously in an amazing way. An increase of adrenalin is released into the bloodstream, which has the effect of enhancing the level of our arousal. A sudden supply of blood to the brain improves our judgement so that we can make decisions much more speedily than usual. The heart beats faster, pumping blood into the muscles so that our body is on 'full alert'. Our breathing rate changes, allowing us access to the necessary supplies of oxygen. Glucose and fats are released into the bloodstream which provide us with additional energy. Our blood pressure rises, drawing the resource from the stomach and intestines. All of this takes place unconsciously and instantaneously, preparing us to encounter whatever it is which is threatening our life. It is an extraordinary happening, for which we can praise God who has so wonderfully and marvellously created us.

All is well as long as the situation we encounter is relatively short in duration. The body has responded magnificently and can now return to its normal, stable situation.

The problems begin to arise when this does not happen, that is, when we remain on 'full alert' for an overlong period of time. Then, instead of enabling us to act positively, the overworked body mechanisms start to have a negative effect. This has been well illustrated by a simple model popularized some years ago by Dr Hans Selye.[4] Naming his model 'The General Adaptation Syndrome', he suggested three phases in our reaction to external threatening situations.

The first phase, the Alarm Reaction, is triggered by an external threat such as we have already noted. This in turn gives rise to the second phase, the Stage of Resistance, which is at a higher level than normal. But if it lasts for too long it moves into the third phase, the

Stage of Exhaustion. In this phase, a whole range of physiological and psychological symptoms start to appear. For example, the muscle tension necessary to meet the emergency becomes discomforting cramp through excessive use. Alertness deteriorates into insomnia. The vital draining of blood from the stomach and intestines soon turns into constipation or diarrhoea. These and many other reactions start to take their toll on our mental capacities which are so closely intertwined with our physical capacities.

Monica is already displaying some of these in her sleeplessness, her irritability and her tearfulness. Those engaged in pastoral care are advised to note these symptoms and those listed below. Caution must be exercised, however, for these symptoms are not exclusively caused by stress.

Physical Symptoms of Stress

- lack of appetite or excessive eating
- frequent indigestion or heartburn
- constipation or diarrhoea
- insomnia
- constant tiredness
- nervous twitches
- nailbiting
- headache
- cramps and muscle spasms
- nausea
- breathlessness without exertion
- tendency to cry
- inability to sit still
- high blood pressure.

Mental Symptoms of Stress

- irritability with people
- inability to cope with everyday things
- lack of interest in life
- constant or recurrent fear of disease
- feeling of failure as a person, a parent, a worker, etc.
- difficulty in making decisions
- loss of interest in other people
- suppressed anger
- inability to show true feelings
- feeling of being the target of other people's animosity
- loss of sense of humour
- feeling of neglect
- dread of the future
- difficulty in concentrating.

The lists, as they stand, are formidable and could be extended. Sadly, these symptoms are becoming increasingly common in contemporary society. The inability to cope with the environmental pressures in which we live and work have taken the place of any life-threatening situations but, unlike the latter, are inclined to be long lasting with disastrous effects.

The Causes of Stress

We will now examine four causes of stress or, as they are usually termed, 'stressors'; namely, life events, work, personality and our Christian faith. The first three, possibly all four, are inter-related but sufficiently different to allow them to be considered separately. They also differ from person to person; what is debilitating for one person may be energizing for another. The emphasis throughout, you will recall, is on the mismatch between the person and his or her environment. As might be expected, particular emphasis will be given in this chapter to the work-related and Christian aspects of stress.

Life Events

Some years ago, two American doctors – Holmes and Rahe – developed a scale which they called the 'Social Readjustment Rating Scale'. They worked on the basis that what really matters about stress is the amount of change it produces in our lives. In conducting their research, they asked participants to assign units to various life events such as marriage, childbirth, bereavement, etc. The end results were not surprising but added a quantitative element to the picture. Thus, the death of a spouse was measured at 100 units, divorce at 73, marriage at 50, change in residence or school at 20 and Christmas at 12.[5]

A number of significant findings emerged from their studies, two of which are particularly interesting. The first was that the stressful impact of these life events could continue for at least 12 months or even more. This is very noticeable in bereavement but may be far less evident in the case of someone who has, for example, moved house. It is important, therefore, that in your work of pastoral care you discover, in a sensitive and appropriate manner, something of the past history of the person who has called for help. Such information can easily be overlooked with unfortunate results.

The second finding was that the stressful impact was cumulative. The 'last straw' might weigh a negligible amount, but when added to the heavy burden already piled on the camel's back it does the damage. Using Holmes and Rahe's scale, therefore, someone who has recently divorced (73 units) and was subsequently dismissed from their job (47 units) is more likely to suffer from stress-related illness than another person who was dismissed at the same time but who enjoys a very stable marriage. Here, then, is another reason for you to get as full an assessment as possible of the person's story.

Turning once more to Monica, we can see already from our brief knowledge of her that there are a number of stressors in her life. Her failing marriage is one; her absent son is another. Indeed, the 'empty nest' situation is frequently a time when a mother encounters pressures hitherto unknown to her. Moreover, it sometimes takes place at the time of the menopause. The financial situation is a further burden that Monica is having to bear, as well as the difficulties at work – which brings us to the next group of stressors.

Work

Holmes and Rahe's research included work-related life events, the highest score of which was dismissal at 47 units followed by retirement (45 units), job change (36 units) and taking on new responsibilities (29 units).

Over the last decade or so, this subject has been widely researched and reported, with publications emanating from government, health authorities, professional institutions, academics and many other agencies. From the ever growing body of knowledge, it is possible to identify five key stressors:

Factors Intrinsic to the Job
There are at least four aspects of work itself which may cause stress.

1. *Lack of control*. Many jobs are highly fragmented, representing part of a process which is seldom understood in its entirety and is usually controlled by someone other than the person doing the work. Such a state of affairs, it will be recalled, was a product of the Enlightenment and the Industrial Revolution (chapter three) and was popularized in the Scientific Management movement (chapter four). The reaction to jobs such as these is often a sense of powerlessness and meaninglessness.

2. *Work overload*. This is a growing feature of life in the 1990s. The recession in many industrial countries in the late '80s and early '90s led to massive reductions in the workforce, with those

remaining after the redundancy programmes having to achieve the same output reached when there were many more people. Those in employment are having to work longer hours and are expected to produce outcomes of the same high quality as before. This adds a further stressful burden to any employee.

3. *Insufficient work.* This can happen at any level, in any job, and is frequently the outcome of technological advance. The airline pilot is a good case in point; the foreman in the process plant who controls everything from a central computer is another. Repetitive routine, boring and understimulating work are major causes of stress.

4. *Physical working environment.* Despite the increase in legislation on this front, unhealthy and unsafe conditions still exist in many offices, shops, factories and other business premises. Noisy, over-crowded and uncomfortable conditions can increase the pressure on individuals and be a source of stress.

Role in the Organization

Two particular aspects of a person's role in an organization are known stressors and are described as role ambiguity and role conflict. Role ambiguity arises when people are unclear about their responsibilities, what is expected of them and how they can obtain adequate information for clarification or direction. Role conflict arises whenever they are expected to achieve mutually contradictory objectives or when they are obliged to carry out work outside their area of responsibility or competence.

Relationships at Work

For many this is the major stressor and can take different forms.

First, there are relationships with superiors. Many managers and supervisors show favouritism, make unnecessarily critical comments about subordinates and take undue advantage of their position. By doing so they create an atmosphere characterized by hostility, tension and distrust – a major stressor.

Then there are relationships with subordinates. The member of the team who is aggressive, unco-operative or unhelpful in any other way can make a supervisor or manager's life distinctly unpleasant. So, too, can the subordinate who is more competent than the person to whom he or she reports.

A third set of potentially stressful relationships are those with colleagues. Difficulties arise from competitiveness, envy, personality clashes, differing views about the fairness of work, responsibilities and rewards. Individuals can be made scapegoats, ignored or given a hard time by others with damaging results to that person's sense of well-being. Two subjects which have received extensive media coverage of late are those of bullying and sexual harassment. Both seem to be on the increase – a sad state of affairs made even worse when it is combined, as it often is, with other kinds of victimization based on racial or religious prejudice.

Security and Status
Redundancy is a major stressor. The impact of redundancy is such that a whole chapter of this book (chapter eight) has been devoted to it. It will come as no surprise that it scores the highest points on Holmes and Rahe's list of work-related causes of stress.

Lack of job security is another stressor. The uncertainty triggered by the experience or fear of redundancy creates in many a sense of helplessness. For the person who has been made redundant it can continue well into the life of a new job. For those who remain with the original employer, it can often result in what is called the 'survivor syndrome' – the feelings of guilt on the part of those who remain in employment. Such guilt is often associated with the fear that their turn will be next.

Another cause is under- or over-promotion. Mental states as extreme as anxiety or depression may arise when an individual is not required to perform to his or her level of competence. It also arises in the person who is promoted above their capability.

Organizational Culture
The word 'culture' is widely used to describe the character of an organization – 'the way things are done here'. It includes all those

characteristics which individually and collectively differentiate one organization from another. People within organizations who find themselves at odds with the culture can be subjected to unmanageable stress. This is particularly the case whenever there is a major change in culture brought about by a takeover, privatization or a new, externally recruited chief executive.

All of these structural stressors are important features to bear in mind when we address the pastoral care of those who suffer from them. So, as once more we recall Monica, we can see two obvious additional causes of stress – the difficulties she is experiencing with her new supervisor and the rumours of takeover.

Personality

Throughout this chapter, we have noted that the same events or situations will often affect different people in different ways. Imagine, for a moment, two people in a train travelling home from work. The train halts between stations and a few minutes later the driver's voice is heard over the loudspeaker system announcing that an engine has broken down further up the line, causing delays to all following trains.

The two people react in very different ways. The first shows annoyance which verges on anger. He walks up and down the carriage criticizing the management of the railway and the gross incompetence of the engineers who have allowed the breakdown to occur. If he has a mobile phone – and such people usually do – he will contact his wife to inform her that 'they' have made another mess, causing him to be late yet again. The other person hardly seems to have noticed the delay. She was reading a book when the train stopped, looked up and around when the announcement was made and resumed her reading thereafter. A shrug of the shoulders and a simple smile suggested indifference to the situation or, more precisely, a realization that she could do nothing about it followed by the decision not to try.

Let us continue to imagine for a moment longer and assume that neither of these two had commitments that evening and were not, therefore, seriously inconvenienced. Why is it that they reacted so differently to the same event? The answer is quite simple – they are different people.

The differences which exist between people have long been a source of fascination to observers of the human condition, already featured in earlier chapters. We will restrict our attention to two aspects of this subject which have a bearing on stress: temperament and conditioned beliefs.

Temperament

Some years ago, two researchers (M. D. Friedman and R. H. Rosenbaum) suggested the co-existence of two personality types simply called A and B.[6] Type A personalities tend to be impatient with others, always wanting to get things done as speedily as possible. They tend to talk and move constantly and rapidly, urging others to adjust to their pace and to do two or more things at the same time. They feel guilty about doing nothing or relaxing. Such personalities, argue Friedman and Rosenbaum, are more prone to stress related illness. Type B personalities, by contrast, seldom suffer from the sense of urgency or impatience as their counterparts. They do not have to impress others with tales of achievements and accomplishments. They enjoy leisurely pastimes and relaxing, and can do both of these with no feelings of guilt. Such people, so the assertion goes, are less prone to stress.

Conditioned Beliefs

It was a saying of the stoic Epictetus that 'Men are not disquieted by things themselves but by their idea of things.' In our story of the train travellers, we noted the very different reactions of two people to the same event. We could conclude that the man was a type A personality and the woman a type B. Another way of addressing the differences is to consider people's belief systems. This is the approach of cognitive behavioural counselling and therapy, which works on the same principle of Epictetus, namely, that it is the interpretation of events rather than the events themselves which impact upon us.

So to return to our travellers. The man may – and it is only may –

unconsciously believe that large organizations like railway companies are incompetent and indifferent to the reactions of their customers. The faulty rolling stock which is the cause of the delay is, by his reckoning, another example of this incompetence and indifference. The woman, by contrast, believes that other people do their best at work and that failure to produce goods and services to meet appropriate needs are outside the control of the individual people concerned. For her, the train delay reinforces that particular belief. As we shall see later, an appropriate strategy for people like our male traveller is to help them examine and change those beliefs which result in disabling behaviour.

And what of Monica? We noted her lack of self-esteem in the opening chapter. Is it due to temperament, belief systems or something entirely different? We do not know, but it could be another cause of stress to her, and she may benefit by being encouraged to look at it.

Christian Faith

The position taken in this chapter, and indeed throughout this book, is that stress in the sense I am using it is negative but not evil. Nor are Christians immune to it, which is the evidence of history and everyday observation. I would go further and argue that there are certain features about being a Christian which can easily contribute to, rather than assist in, coping with stress; namely, confused beliefs and the pressure to conform.

Confused Beliefs
Some Christians experience stress on account of their beliefs about moral behaviour. The experience of such Christians is that, although they sincerely proclaim a gospel of grace, they feel obliged to live according to the rule of law. The words 'must' and 'should' occur frequently in their conversation. They suffer, as the saying goes, from a hardening of the 'oughteries'. For such Christians, life can become particularly stressful when they find their previously held views are

no longer supported by others.

This has happened in recent years in the realms of sexual behaviour, of marriage and divorce, of inter-faith dialogue, of women priests and many other subjects. For some, the challenge to existing views is a stimulus but for others it can be a source of considerable stress.

Other Christians experience stress arising from their beliefs about emotional states. The well known hymn by J. G. Whittier contains the verse:

> Drop thy still dews of quietness
> Till all our strivings cease.
> Take from our souls the strain and stress
> And let our ordered lives confess
> The beauty of thy peace.

There is an implicit suggestion in this verse that the Christian is somehow immune to the afflictions which are encountered by other people or, if not immune, certainly has a way of escape. The person who follows Christ, it could be concluded, need only look to him and a state of tranquillity is assured. Such a view is contained in Patsy Kettle's booklet *Staying Sane Under Stress*.[7] For her, the very action of saying or singing these words results in the strivings actually ceasing:

> The still dews of quietness are given, replacing the strain and stress that make up my disordered life. Gradually the peace comes, the beauty of his peace.[8]

This is in marked contrast to the views of another Christian writer, the psychiatrist Gaius Davies, who considers that the quiet hope expressed by the hymn writer is at odds with 'the conflict and striving which the Bible describes as part of the fight of faith (and indeed of life itself).'[9] Davies' view is that the sort of serenity promised in the hymn is contrary to the pressures which Christians encounter as 'they fight manfully against the world, the flesh and the devil.'

Whether we incline to the view of Patsy Kettle or Gaius Davies, it is important that a right understanding is held on such key Christian subjects as joy and peace. Confused beliefs, particularly on these topics, so easily engender added stress. What is more, the Christian who believes he or she should have peace and does not experience it is so easily inclined to feel a failure or to experience guilt. A vicious circle then ensues.

Pressure to Conform

The New Testament abounds in collective metaphors describing the people of God – a household, a royal priesthood, a family, a nation, a body. Each metaphor adds something special to our understanding and experience of being part of a whole, yet each implicitly or explicitly asserts differences. This is particularly so in the case of the body metaphor where the multi-faceted, yet inter-related, aspects of believers' gifts are applauded and affirmed. Sadly, though, this biblical emphasis is not always remembered when Christians gather together and the pressure for conformity becomes an issue. Obviously, the importance of conformity needs to be recognized. Orthodoxy, a word which literally means right thinking or belief, is the chief bastion against heresy. Credal statements demonstrating the commonality of Christian beliefs are fundamental. There comes a time, however, when the sameness of thought, action and experience denies the diversity recognized in the New Testament and results in individual Christians feeling under stress.

This often happens without any intention on the part of the Christian community concerned. We see it sometimes when one or, more often, several members of a church have experienced God in a very special way. A dramatic conversion, perhaps, or a second blessing, or a mystical experience. The group who have a shared experience broadcast it to their fellow Christians. The minister at the church may even encourage them to say something about it at a particular service. Thus far, all is well. God is glorified as others tell of his blessings outpoured on them. But then something insidious starts to happen. The experience which was shared by the small group is commended to the wider church community. Soon there is a suggestion that the experience is normative for all Christians and then, sadly, it is put forward as prescriptive for those who are fully committed – or some such other value-laden phrase – to Christ. Those who have not had such an experience can – at first – rejoice, but if the pattern summarized above is followed begin to feel that their own experience is somewhat lacking. Doubt creeps in, and what was a source of thanksgiving soon becomes a source of doubt. And doubt is frequently the companion of stress.

Monica comes to mind again, for it will be recalled from our very first chapter that she saw herself as a second-rate Christian. How can we help her?

Strategies for Pastoral Care

What sort of pastoral care can be offered to those whose stress – like Monica's – is partly, if not wholly, derived from work-related activities? There are, of course, no universal answers, no panacea that can be offered to all with the certainty of success. There are a number of approaches, however, that we can adopt which may well enable Monica – and others like her – to manage the stress (in the first, neutral, sense of the word) she encounters so that her life becomes far less subject to stress (in the second, negative, sense of the word). These strategies can be divided into two groups: the first is mainly concerned with the causes of stress, the stressors; the second with the symptoms of stress and individual pastoral care.

The Stressors

This section is directed towards those in leadership positions within the Church. Comments are of a general nature, setting the appropriate environment against which support can be given. Actions are suggested which are under the direct control of the minister and apply to all in his or her care, whether or not such people are known to be suffering from stress.

The first point to be made is a plea to those who exercise a preaching and teaching ministry, that they demonstrate sensitivity when dealing with the subjects of peace and joy, anxiety and depression. Considerable harm has been done to those who receive a clear message from the pulpit that peace and joy are guaranteed states for the Christian. Similarly, there are many who, struggling with anxiety or depression, hear sermons which suggest that there must be something amiss with their relationship with God. Ministers might consider a series of sermons on characters from the Bible and Church history to whose mental struggles we would nowadays give the title 'stress'. Jeremiah is a good example; Martin Luther, another. Some of St Paul's writings include highly relevant material, as do some classic Christian autobiographies and biographies.

A second plea addressed to all in leadership positions is to avoid the imposition of excessive demands and expectations on church members. The old adage which says that if you want a job done well, you need to find a busy person, is an attractive one because of its practicality. There comes a point, however, and it is often spotted far too late, when that person's busyness becomes an overwhelming burden.

A third stress-inducing practice, which is often adopted with the best of motives, is to enforce a particular form of spirituality on the whole congregation or church membership. We are different people with diverse gifts, and God deals with us in the way he chooses. To suggest that another person's experience of God is invalid is not only insensitive, it is also wrong. To encourage others to pursue a different spiritual journey from the one on which they know God is directing them is the sign of the false shepherd.

A fourth stressor is that of change. The contemporary world of work is one of continuous change which frequently results in feelings of insecurity. Christians facing problems in this part of their lives are seldom helped by full-scale changes introduced into the church in which they have worshipped for many years. Those in leadership, knowingly or otherwise, can increase or relieve the stress on those committed to their care.

From these pleas for wise and sensitive treatment of others, let me make two practical suggestions. The first is an extension of the call to preach on the subject; recognizing, however, that preaching may not always be the most appropriate vehicle. An alternative is a programme on stress management which, if handled well, might become a form of outreach to others as well as a service to those within the church. The second suggestion for those in leadership is to maintain a list of resources. From within or outside the church membership, discover who can provide help; then evaluate the quality of that resource and, finally, put it to good use.

Individual Pastoral Care

This second grouping is for those engaged in pastoral care, and is about remedial responses rather than preventive interventions. This section sets out a range of actions which might be taken by the person suffering from stress, and as such provides the counsellor with a sort of toolkit from which the appropriate instrument can be selected to meet the person's need.

Being in a highly stressed situation makes it hard for someone to think clearly and to choose. Moreover, he or she is often unaware of the many simple approaches which can have such a fundamental impact. The advice, therefore, is offered to you, the pastoral carer, for you to choose whenever and wherever appropriate. First of all, it is important to discover the sources of stress.

Identify the Stressors

As we have seen, stress of the negative sort may be caused by life events, by work, by personality, by faulty Christian beliefs or the pressure to conform to one pattern of spirituality. It is quite likely that more than one stressor is involved. You can discover the causes by careful questioning and listening. A formal and very practical questionnaire can be used, such as the Occupational Stress Indicator[10] which takes into account the many stressors listed above. Whatever approach you adopt, work hard to get the diagnosis right. Then you can choose the appropriate interventions.

A Balanced Lifestyle

The person who adopts a balanced lifestyle is less prone to stress than the person given to excess or paucity, the exception occurring when a particular lifestyle becomes an obsession in itself. The combination of a sensible diet, moderate physical exercise and regular sleep lays a good foundation for managing stress. The first two are in most people's control, although medical advice should be taken before undertaking any major change programme. The third may not be so easy. Parents may be disturbed frequently by their young children. Moreover, sleeplessness is often a symptom itself of stress and this certainly seems outside the person's ability to change. Sometimes, however, it can be controlled; for example, in the case of those who have got into the habit of going to bed very late for no other reason than that they have always done so.

Appropriate Levels of Activity

Linked to lifestyle is a person's level of activity. There are those who go through life as though they have their foot hard down on the accelerator. This is a characteristic of the Type A personality we saw earlier. It is also a characteristic of those Christians who support their frenzied activity by reference to the New Testament metaphors of military service or athletic competition. Just as a car engine performs badly when subjected continually to maximum revolutions per minute, so the body – the temple of the Holy Spirit – can often react in a debilitated manner. The discipline of keeping a stress diary and of deliberately switching off can be an antidote. Presented in the right way, such a discipline can be made attractive to the 'driven' person, who will see it as something else to achieve!

Have a Break

Rest, like work, was ordained by God as part of his plan for humankind. We neglect it at our peril and do disservice to God at the same time. Rest as a regular pattern is absolutely vital if we are to honour God. Christians who are as active on Sundays as on every other day of the week, may find themselves becoming stressed beyond their capabilities. It is sometimes hard for ministers to accept that immensely talented people, who might contribute to church-centred activities, 'only' worship God on Sundays. It may be that this is the only way they can use their talents most effectively for God at all other times.

A break is as good as a rest, so the saying goes, provided it is not confused with patterned rest ordained by God. The annual holiday, the weekend away or the retreat can provide the right answer to stress for some. (All of these, of course, have a financial tab; this is where other Christians can help those who are suffering from stress on account of money problems.) Or it may be doing something entirely different – at home or away, alone or with others, physical or mental.

Being in Control

Many people suffering from stress feel overwhelmed and totally out of control. While there are certain situations over which they can have no control they are seldom as powerless as they feel. Planning the day can be helpful for such people, with emphasis given to establishing priorities and monitoring progress.

There is a well-known prayer which adorns the walls of many homes and reads:

Grant me the serenity to accept things I cannot change,
Courage the things I can
And wisdom to know the difference.[11]

Adopting a realistic approach to control can be a major step on the road to managing stress. Devoting energy to matters outside our control is not only a futile exercise, it adds to the burdens we already carry. Realism is also important in terms of achievement. Setting targets which are beyond the person's reach is likely to induce stress whenever failure occurs, as it undoubtedly will.

Support Systems

Stress can be magnified if kept private. Christians can be helped by their fellow Christians in ways which have already been mentioned.

There are others, too, who might be able to assist; the stressed person can be encouraged to make a list of them with the help of you, the carer. These might include family, friends, GP, people at work, neighbours and counsellors. Those suffering from stress may be disinclined to 'bother other people with my problems'. They are often surprised to learn of the many resources, in the shape of people, that they already have available to them.

Adaptive Behaviour

The Type A personality can learn to behave differently as a means of reducing stress. So, too, can the person who always feels 'put upon'. Acquiring new behaviour patterns (for example, assertiveness or listening skills), is in the capacity of us all except for the very few whose stress levels have precipitated severe mental conditions, which call for psychiatric help. You can often act as mentor or coach in helping others in these areas.

New Attitudes

Much stress is brought about because of the way we interpret events or the behaviour of others. We reach conclusions which have a damaging effect on our own self-esteem which may be wholly unjustified or untrue. The renewal of the mind is a fundamental part of the Christian's journey (Romans 12:2). It is also a powerful antidote to stress.

Expressing Emotions

Stress increases in direct proportion to the quantity of emotional containment practised by the individual. This may not be a precise formula resulting from empirical research but it contains a lot of good sense. Laughter and tears, if allowed a free rein, can relieve those tensions experienced by many people suffering from stress. So, too, can anger although some self-discipline may have to be exercised if the physical manifestations become extreme.

Relaxation

The stressed person finds it hard, if not impossible, to relax and, therefore, needs help. There is a lot of such help available and you are advised to become familiar with some of the exercises which can be used. These are described in many books and delivered on many programmes. Some of them, however, are based on beliefs about human nature which are at odds with Christian beliefs. A positive approach might therefore be to link relaxation with meditation and prayer.

Appropriate Prayer

The subtitle of Richard Foster's book on prayer[12] is 'Finding the heart's true home'. Stress often results when people feel alienated, isolated and unloved. They lack the warm, supporting comfort of the true home. Prayer can meet that need but only if it is appropriate prayer. There are many factors which determine the appropriateness of particular forms of prayer and there is no neat formula which can supply the answer. Richard Foster describes 21 discrete forms of prayer which have been honoured throughout time among Christian traditions. Those which are associated with meditation and contemplation are likely to be much more appropriate to a stressed person than those which are accompanied by an outburst of triumphalist praise. Consider the use of these and adopt, for example, the approach suggested by the Jesuit writer, Anthony de Mello.[13]

As pastoral carers, seek to develop the attitude of the spiritual director in travelling with the stressed disciple of Christ on his or her journey. Monica will continue to be encumbered by money matters, concerned about Alf and Darren, and worried by the uncertainties of her job. She will know, however, that all these stressors can be managed as she is accompanied by you on her pilgrimage to a safe haven, the heart's true home.

7

IDENTITY, SELF-ESTEEM
AND WORK

You have made him a little lower than the heavenly beings.
(Psalm 8:5)

The next character we meet is Christine, the curate's wife.

Christine's Story

Christine graduated from university with a first-class
honours degree in economics. She then stayed on a further
year studying for a masters degree, for which her disserta-
tion was on sustainable agricultural policies in Central
African countries. Several of her fellow students on the
masters course were Africans and most of them were
Christians. Their lifestyle and their infectious enthusiasm
revealed to Christine a great void in her own life and she
herself became a Christian.

These same African colleagues introduced her to James
who attended a church in the city where she studied, and
whose parents adopted an open-house policy for any young
people – predominantly overseas students – who wanted to
share in family life. James and Christine were mutually
attracted from the outset and they saw a lot of each other in
the last few months of her studies. It seemed only natural

that they should get married soon after she completed her masters degree.

Christine found a job with an international aid agency based once more in the university city – a 'God-send', as both James and she termed it. The open style of the organization gave her the opportunity to articulate her views and soon she found herself able to test the practicability of some of the theoretical ideas she had evolved during her post-graduate studies. She was helped considerably by some of her erstwhile student colleagues, who had returned to take up important appointments in their home country government departments. Her considerable intelligence, her specialist knowledge and her contacts, allied to her Christian compassion for the poor, enabled her to flourish in the aid agency. By the end of two years she was writing articles for professional journals, attending meetings with government representatives and had been invited to speak at a major conference. Christine loved her work and felt fulfilled and valued in it.

It was just after her conference address – which had been well received – that James had told her he was seriously considering ordination. This was something of a shock for Christine; she knew that he was not happy in his work but considered that it could be easily rectified by a change of job. Slowly, however, she grew accustomed to the idea. Indeed, she started to become enthusiastic when they talked about the possibility of inner-city work or even a move to Africa.

During James' time at theological college, Christine continued working with the aid agency, winning a public reputation for herself as a critic of what she considered to be misguided overseas development policies on the part of the British government. She also spent time with the African students at James' college, exploring with them how they might combine their church responsibilities with the agricultural needs of their home countries.

James' acceptance of a curacy in middle-class suburbia

was an unwelcome surprise to Christine, for it held out none of the challenges she had hoped for in an inner-city parish. Worst of all, it meant leaving her job, since James' new appointment was three hours' drive away from the agency. With great reluctance and considerable annoyance, she moved to their new home and their new church.

At first, she was very unhappy but then found two good friends in Sally and the vicar's wife, Anne. Sally, who had a husband as dogmatic as her own, made her laugh and guaranteed her sanity. Anne, who had had no formal education beyond school, was widely read, extremely wise and ensured her mind did not degenerate. Christine also made some good friends at the local supporters group of the aid agency and led, on their behalf, what they jokingly referred to as the 'persecution of their neo-fascist member of parliament'.

At the time of the meeting they had been in the parish for eighteen months. James was very happy but Christine was not. Despite her friendship with Sally and Anne she felt she was losing her sense of identity and, with it, any sense of self-worth. She had become the curate's wife and was expected to do things which she neither agreed with nor enjoyed. She felt that the congregation of the church were alternately condescending towards her or critical of her.

Then the letter arrived from the agency. They had been loaned an office in London for three years. Could Christine work there for two or three days a week? She was overjoyed and phoned Sally straightaway who, needless to say, was absolutely delighted and thought she should accept the offer immediately. James, however, did not share her enthusiasm. He believed that God had called them both to parish work and he wanted Christine's support for his activities. The row that followed was the worst they had had since they were married. Christine was James' intellectual superior and could always defeat him in rational debate, but he could play what she and Sally called the 'God-card' with consummate skill. God's will must be done ... Christine's call was to be the curate's wife.

Christine felt utterly dejected. She knew she had many talents which could be used most effectively in the aid agency yet she was required to abandon that course of action in pursuit of something far less worthwhile.

Identity and Self-Esteem

Christine probably has a number of issues to confront in her life but the two on which we will now concentrate are the related ones of identity and self-esteem. She is not alone in facing these issues, for Frank is in a similar position and so, perhaps, are others at the meeting. And so, too, are many who look to us for pastoral care, especially those who are unemployed; as we shall see, work impacts strongly both on identity and on self-esteem in our society. Before putting forward working definitions for these issues, however, I want to consider the much more complex concept of the self.

The Self

The idea of the self is as old as Western philosophy. From the sixth century BC, Greek philosophers used the word 'psyche' (often translated as 'soul' in English) to express a key concept in their thinking. The concept is the existence in humankind of something which encapsulates man's being. Psyche, as one writer puts it, is 'the epitome of the individual ... the self, or the seat of moral and spiritual qualities.'[1] It embraces a person's thoughts, emotions and will. In Greek philosophy – and that of many later thinkers influenced by its ideas – this self is distinct from the body which houses it; hence came the belief that although the body disintegrates, the soul is immortal.

Subsequent Western philosophers introduced a new perspective on the self. It was that the inner workings of the self often pose difficulties for a person from which they cannot escape. So, for example, the Epicurean poet Lucretius, writing in the first century BC observes:

> *Each man flies from his own self; yet from that self he has no power to escape.*[2]

Herein lies the theoretical seed of what was to blossom two millennia later in the writings of William James, Sigmund Freud and the other founders of modern psychology. In the intervening period, however, the seed did not lie dormant. It was, like much else besides, rediscovered at the Renaissance and developed intellectually in the fruitful soil of the Enlightenment and beyond. In one dictionary of pastoral theology, R. S. Anderson highlights this development through the writings of the philosophers Descartes, Locke, Hume and Hegel.[3] In another dictionary, this time devoted to pastoral care, Warwick Ross shows how the philosophers' idea was taken up by the psychologists Freud, Jung, Adler, Gordon Allport, Carl Rogers and Erich Fromm.[4]

Despite the widespread espousal of the concept by philosophers and psychologists alike, there is no definition which is universally accepted or sufficiently comprehensive to cover the wide diversity of views which have been propounded over the centuries. You may, therefore, ask why we need to bother about it at all. The simple answer is that without a biblical perspective we can all so easily fall into the trap of false teaching and false values. Later in this chapter we shall be examining some of the words which incorporate self, such as self-fulfilment and self-actualization, and examine them in the light of scripture. For the moment, I want to dwell briefly on the Christian concept of self. Two key characteristics are to be noted.

The first is that the Bible does not recognize the distinction between body and soul which is implicit or explicit in many of the premises of philosophers and psychologists. In chapter two we noted that the Hebrew and Greek words variously translated as body, soul, spirit and mind are used interchangeably to describe the person. The Bible insists on a holistic view of humankind.

The second is that the person can only be understood in relation to others – to other human beings, to the created order and, principally, to God. Whereas ancient and contemporary non-Christian writers are concerned with escaping from themselves or finding themselves or fulfilling themselves, the biblical emphasis is on encountering God. Compare, for example, the stanza from Lucretius' poem quoted above with the words of the psalmist a few centuries earlier:

Where can I go from your spirit?
Where can I flee from your presence?
If I go up to the heavens, you are there;
If I make my bed in the depths, you are there.
If I rise on the wings of dawn,
If I settle on the far side of the sea,
Even there your hand will guide me,
Your right hand will hold me fast. (Psalm 139:7–10)

The story of the Fall in Genesis 3 is the story of humankind seeking autonomy and independence. The temptation to which Adam and the woman succumbed was to be 'like God' or 'as gods' (Genesis 3:5).[5] Their desire, so often like ours, was for self-sufficiency. It is a quality which is accorded high value in many Western societies and influences parenting, education, financial management and much else besides. Because of this, Christians who engage in pastoral care need to beware of the emphases of secular counselling and psychotherapy which highlight individuality to the exclusion of other aspects. We do well to remember the opening words of St Augustine's *Confessions* which proclaim that 'our hearts [by which Augustine meant the whole person, the self] are restless until they find their rest in you.'[6]

How, then, can we understand the self or selfhood as Christians? The key lies in the writings of one of the earliest Christian writers, Irenaeus, who in his great work *Adversus Haereses* made a distinction between carnal man and spiritual man.[7] The former is one who separates the soul or the self from God and is thereby less than human. Heather Ward is much influenced by Irenaeus in her book *The Gift of Self*.[8] She writes of selfhood as being 'the capacity for God'[9] and later as 'the receptivity within us which turns outwards to God in acceptance of life as a gift'.[10] Christian writers such as Christopher Bryant and Bruce Duncan, who have been greatly influenced by the works of Carl Jung, make a similar distinction. Bryant explains the Jungian concept of the archetype of the self, which encourages men and women to realize their fullest potential. He adds that the gospel 'crowns the insight' of the psychologist by proclaiming that, for each person, God has set 'eternity in his heart', calling us to recognize that what is achieved in this life is only part of the journey which will be completed in the world to come.[11]

Bruce Duncan asserts that the ego-centred self of the secular psychologist is different from the self of Christian teaching, which is the 'indwelling Christ, hallowing and transforming your life'.[12] Leanne Payne, despite her dislike of Jung, makes the same point when she describes the new self as having 'one face, turned up to God, seeing and hearing with singleness of heart', a new self which has 'the capacity to communicate with the Father'.[13]

All these writers emphasize the same distinction in different ways. It is simply captured in some words from Thomas Merton which affirm that the self is 'not its own centre and does not orbit around itself; it is centred on God, the one centre of all'.[14] It is Merton's definition of the self which I shall adopt.

Identity and Self-Esteem – A Working Definition

I have used the words identity and self-esteem on a number of occasions already in this book, on the assumption that they convey a more-or-less common meaning to the reader. Now that we are focusing specifically on them, however, a working definition is called for.

Identity is the answer to the question 'Who am I?'. Self-esteem is the response provoked in the person by the answer to that question.

Self-esteem, which is considered here as synonymous with self-acceptance or self-worth, might be positive or negative, high or low. Positive or high self-esteem is neatly rendered by that much-used phrase of Thomas Harris, 'I'm OK.'[15] It represents an experience of satisfaction and contentment with the image I hold of myself and the image, as far as I am aware, of that held of me by others. Negative or low self-esteem is the reverse. It is akin to the 'inferiority complex' introduced into our vocabulary by Alfred Adler. It is a dissatisfaction with the way I perceive myself in relation to my own self-image and in relation to the views held of me by others.

The Development of Identity

In this section, I will concentrate on the stages in a person's life, and the links between those stages and identity and self-esteem. The three stages are childhood, adolescence and adulthood. In this I will draw heavily on the work of Erik Erikson,[16] whose model of the Eight Ages of Man has had an enormous impact on the understanding of human development and has influenced many subsequent writers, including Christians such as Donald Capps,[17] James Fowler,[18] Michael Jacobs[19] and Frank Lake.[20] It was Erikson who first coined the phrase 'identity crisis'; his model seeks to explain that at each stage of a person's development a 'crisis' has to be resolved, the outcome of which determines his or her ability to manage the changing demands within themselves and the society in which they move. The negotiation of this crisis greatly influences the person's identity and describes the part they are able to play in society.

Erikson's Model

Erikson uses the psychosexual language of Freud to introduce the early stages of a person's development and then throws in a few words of his own to encompass the periods following adolescence. He argues that negotiations of each of these stages contribute significantly to the development of particular characteristics in the person. The stages are represented by way of what Erikson called an 'epigenetic chart'[21] but lend themselves to simple verbal descriptions:

First Stage: Oral/Sensory

The initial stage of a person's life is characterized by intimate contact with one other person, usually the mother. The outcome of these early months, if the contact is good, results in a sense of trust; if not, of mistrust.

Second Stage: Muscular/Anal

This is the first experience of 'holding on' or 'letting go', parodied in the popular imagination as potty training. Successful negotiation results in a sense of autonomy; unsuccessful in shame and doubt.

Third Stage: Locomotor/Genital

Children begin to move without assistance from an adult at this stage. They also take a considerable interest in their genitalia. The way they are assisted through this results in a sense of initiative or of guilt which may follow them through life.

Fourth Stage: Latency

These are early school days where the child moves, for the first time, away from the protection of the home. If they succeed at this stage, they will develop a sense of industry; if not, a sense of inferiority.

Fifth Stage: Puberty and Adolescence

Childhood ends here and youth starts. These are the teenage years of rapid change, both physically and emotionally. A successful outcome of this stage creates a strong sense of identity; an unsuccessful one results in role confusion.

Sixth Stage: Young Adulthood

Identification with others or one other person is a feature during this period. So, too, is competitiveness. The results of this stage are either intimacy or isolation.

Seventh Stage: Adulthood

This is the time associated with setting up home, having a family, earning a living for oneself and others. It is the lengthiest stage and is influenced by the successful or unsuccessful resolution of all the others. Its outcome is either generativity (a word which embraces productivity and creativity) or stagnation.

Eighth Stage: Maturity
The final stage, which culminates either in ego-integrity or in despair.

Having sketched out Erikson's model, let us turn to the three key stages which impact on self-esteem and identity. In negotiating these, other people have a significant impact. Usually they are different people at each stage, a reality which some parents find difficult to accept.

Childhood

The greatest influence on the child is its parents, be they natural, step, adoptive or foster. Through the responses from the parents, children learn whether certain activities and emotions are good or bad. They also learn – and this is the crucial issue in this context – whether they are deemed good or bad. It is during childhood and as a result of parental attitudes and behaviours that children first discover whether they are of value, whether they are OK. Herein lie the origins of positive or negative self-esteem. Other children, particularly siblings, also have an influence but it is a minor one unless – and this happens not infrequently in contemporary society – an elder child is required to act *in loco parentis* because mother and father are not available.

Adolescence

As we noted in our quick trip through Erikson's eight stages, adolescence is the time that a person has to face up to the identity crisis. Parents continue to have some influence but it is a diminishing, often painful, one as children assert themselves and deliberately rebel against mother or father or both. Parental influence is replaced by that of two other groups. The first consists of the teenager's peers.

Acceptance by the peer group is of enormous importance to the adolescents. Such acceptance often displays itself in conformity of dress, in behaviour and in moral standards. The second influence is one or more significant adults. They may be people with whom the young person has frequent contact such as a teacher, a youth leader, a neighbour or a family friend. Or they may be the heroes or heroines of the worlds of entertainment, sport or some other activity which is valued by the person and probably the group.

Adulthood

Emerging from adolescence, a person will have faced up to the crisis of identity. He or she will either have a clear answer to the question 'Who am I?' or will still be confused. In the adulthood stage yet more actors join the cast list of influences with three groups representing various degrees of importance. For the married person, it is the partner who contributes most to that determinant of self-esteem called by two Christian authors the Love of Another.[22] The partner also contributes to another of their criteria, namely, the Performance of Roles,[23] for marriage enables the person to engage in the tasks of parenthood, breadwinner, homemaker and many others besides. The major influences that come from work colleagues, and fellow Christians (particularly those who worship together in the same church) will be explored later in the chapter.

We shall now investigate the sources of negative and positive self-esteem, looking at two major contributors to both areas; pastoral carers can use the latter to prevent or counter the former.

Sources of Negative Self-Esteem

The Confusion between Having, Doing and Being

During the 1970s, Erich Fromm wrote a book entitled *To Have or To Be?*.[24] In it, he demonstrated two ways of existence that characterize human societies and the people who live in them. The 'having' way is characterized by acquisitiveness, competitiveness and destruction; the 'being' way, in contrast, is characterized by shared experience, productive activity and the ascendency of human over material values. He argued that the values of any society are more likely to influence those of the individual rather than the other way round.

Western societies are characterized, according to Fromm, by the 'having' way and, in consequence, considerable value is attached to those who have. Those who do not have, in the sense of wealth, health, possessions, jobs, etc., can easily perceive themselves as lesser persons than those who do. Identity and self-esteem, therefore, often get confused by the failure to separate having from being.

They can also be confused by failing to separate being from doing. Those familiar with Neuro-Linguistic Programming[25] will recognize the phrase, 'logical levels'. It suggests that meaning can be characterized under five different headings. This is illustrated by taking the sentence 'I can't do that here' and placing the emphasis successively on each word. Thus:

'I' indicates identity and responds to the word 'Who?'

'can't' talks about beliefs and values using the word 'Why?'

'do' introduces capability and the question 'How?'

'that' refers to behaviour employing the word 'What?'

'here' talks of environment addressing the questions 'When?' and 'Where?'.

For many people, capability and behaviour get confused with identity. Negative self-esteem is produced because what I do or how I do it is perceived as unsatisfactory, and this translates itself into my very identity. My doing takes over from my being and I see myself as unsatisfactory.

Living with Unrealistic Expectations

Closely linked with this is the way we view ourselves in the light of our own and others' experiences. Joanna and Alister McGrath remind us of the cognitive-behavioural theory which I introduced in chapter six.[26] This suggests that our valuation of ourself is influenced not by the events or the people we encounter but by the way we interpret those events and those encounters. That interpretation may have been influenced in childhood, adolescence or later but it is one which we carry about with us for most of our life. It evidences itself in expressions such as 'I ought to', 'I must' and 'I have to'. Our self-esteem will be influenced by what we believe is expected of us.

Sources of Positive Self-Esteem

Acceptance

'You don't know how much you have helped me' is a frequent comment made by those who have been able to express their views to a willing listener. The listener is often perplexed because he or she seems to have done little by way of offering advice or extending help. What has happened, of course, is the person who has done all the talking has felt accepted by the listener. For many people this is not a common experience. They may have been rejected in childhood, in adolescence or through adulthood and their sense of self-esteem is minimal. Those who have grown up in an accepting family, an accepting school, with an accepting partner and among accepting colleagues are much more likely to have positive self-esteem.[27]

Affirmation

I have worked, for many years, with chartered accountants who, when they discharge their role as auditors, are required to uncover any shortcomings of the management of those companies whose shareholders they represent. Unfortunately, many of us, regardless of our occupation, are better at finding fault than giving praise. The person who is affirmed from childhood onwards as a person of value is much more likely to experience positive self-esteem than the person who is constantly put down.

The Influence of Work on Identity and Self-Esteem

In the course of this chapter, I have made mention of the roles performed by people several times. Let us look at five key areas in which work has a profound impact on a person's identity and self-esteem:

Relationships with Others

We have all found ourselves using the work which we do or the role we perform as a means of introducing ourself to others. 'I am a graphic designer'; 'I work in the computer industry'; 'I am employed by ABC plc'. It is such an important indicator of identity that retired people still refer back to what they used to do. They may say, 'I was a secretary for many years'; they may hold on to the title which described their work, such as doctor, colonel or bishop. Or, and this applies exclusively to clergy, they may continue to wear the clerical collar.

Economic Independence

Competence, and with it a sense of self-esteem, is supported by having appropriate financial means. People in such a position will often express the view that they are not 'beholden to anyone' or that they can 'stand on their own two feet'.

Control

This relates to the previous area but is wider, for it covers the structuring of time even though that structure is imposed by others.

Contribution to Society

A person is often seen as giving in some way or other rather than receiving through work. The very fact that they pay taxes means that they are supporting those who do not.

Exercise of Abilities

Work provides many people with the opportunities to use their talents and to develop new skills. This, in turn, adds to their feeling of competence – a regular companion of self-esteem.

Work, then, plays a fundamental part in establishing identity and nurturing positive self-esteem.

The Effect of Negative Self-Esteem

Those who have no employment work – and see no hope of finding any – face a titanic struggle to enjoy those characteristics associated with high self-esteem. Monica's husband, Alf, is an all too typical example. He is becoming increasingly isolated and belligerent; he hates being dependent on his wife and having no influence of his own; he has nothing to give and can only lament the passing of better times.

These are not the only symptoms of negative self-esteem and I have reproduced a few more in the list below. But just as I warned of the danger, when we looked at the effects of stress, of associating the list exclusively with stress, so the same is true here. Negative self-esteem may produce some of the following symptoms but they may be caused by other features. Therefore, let us proceed with caution. Low self-esteem is frequently associated with:

lack of confidence

indecisiveness

feelings of failure

difficulties in making relationships

blaming others

anger.

It can also lead to personality disorders which, in turn, trigger mental illness which might be as extreme as anxiety disorders, paranoid delusions or depression.[28]

Negative self-esteem is a powerful force. We have seen its effect on Christine and glimpsed it in Frank, Monica and Sally, and maybe in Peter. How can Christians respond? Does the Bible throw light on the subject? If it does, can we use it in our pastoral care? The answer to both the latter questions is definitely 'Yes'. We will, therefore, complete this section by highlighting the biblical view and then devote the final section to strategies for pastoral care.

The Biblical View

Those who have read the writings of Frank Lake or the book on self-esteem by Joanna and Alister McGrath will recognize my indebtedness to these authors. I will start with Frank Lake's 'Dynamic Cycle',[29] adding my own commentary where appropriate.

Lake developed his model as a means of correlating our experience of Christ, as authenticated by the scriptures, with our knowledge of the theories of human development. He made a starting point of focusing on the 'well-functioning personality and of spiritual health'[30] rather than on personality disorders on the one hand, and sin on the other. In today's jargon his approach would be defined as 'solution-based' rather than 'problem-based'.

Lake's model is a complex one but can be visually imagined as a clockface with four equidistant steps around the dial. These he calls acceptance (12 o'clock), sustenance (3 o'clock), status or significance (6 o'clock) and achievement (9 o'clock). The first step, acceptance, is the source of identity. It depends, in the earliest days of childhood, on the mutually satisfactory relationship between a giving mother and a responsive baby. The second step, sustenance, continues the sense of being through the mother's giving of herself. Lake calls these first two steps the 'input phase'. The third step, significance, represents the beginning of self-consciousness and provides the support for sound relationships. It makes the move from 'being' to 'well-being'. The fourth step is that of achievement which embraces learning in young life and performance or service later on. These two steps are called the 'output phase'. The cycle continues into the acceptance phase once more but as the person ages, the relationships which can nurture it change from parent to significant others.

The model, which is psychoanalytic in origin, is compatible with the successful negotiation of Erikson's stages and reinforces the importance of acceptance and affirmation. Disorder sets in when the cycle is reversed at any point; for example, when significance is thought to be dependent upon achievement rather than the other way round. When this happens, both the well-being and the being, the self-esteem and the identity, are damaged.

Lake goes on to demonstrate that this cycle is fully revealed in the gospel accounts of Jesus Christ. Jesus is accepted by his Father (Matthew 3:17) and gains his sustenance by abiding in him (John 1:18). He realizes his significance as he goes out to others, on the grounds of his association with the Father (John 8:23;10:36) and achieves the Father's work of redemption through his life, death and resurrection (John 4:34;16:5;17:4;19:30).

A biblical view of self-esteem incorporates the basic tenets of Christian faith. Our self-esteem is not dependent upon our achievements, nor on our role. It rests exclusively on God's grace. It starts with an awareness that God has created us 'a little lower than the heavenly beings and crowned with glory and honour' and that he has made us for the purpose of exercising dominion as his representative over his whole creation (Psalm 8). It continues with the recognition that we are sinful in God's eyes and deserve the consequences of sin, but rejoices to realize God's provision of a way of escape through the death of his Son. This intervention by God flows from his love and is entirely of grace. Thus it is made possible for us to become his sons and daughters and, through the work of the Holy Spirit, grow into the fullness of Christ. The self-image (a word preferred by Anthony Hoekema in preference to self-esteem), having been perverted, is now renewed into the image of God.[31]

And our identity? We cannot, in the judgement of Paul Tournier, give a doctrinaire answer to this fundamental question.[32] What we can understand is that we are accepted and sustained by the Trinity, and that acceptance and sustenance is ever present and available to us as we seek God's kingdom.

Strategies for Pastoral Care

How can we help those, like Christine, who are suffering from low self-esteem, which is brought on (just as in her case) by the inability to do the work for which they are so well suited? How can we help Monica's husband and son, who can find no sense of self-worth owing to their long-term unemployment? Once again, there are no neat answers, for these are complex issues, but there are some steps that you can take which can be of great assistance.

The Importance of Acceptance

The apostle James roundly condemns his fellow Christians, who judge a person by his or her outward appearance and offer hospitality in proportion to the impression created by the visitor (James 3:2–4). Make sure you do not fall into the same trap! The unlovely needs the love and acceptance which you can give more than the person who is usually in a state of well-being.

The Power of Affirmation

A middle-aged man comes for counselling. The previous minister at the church he attends had encouraged his participation in youthwork. He may not have contributed much to the success of that work but the affirmation he received from the minister, and the youth leaders, worked wonders for his self-esteem. He began to recover from many years of being told that he was a failure. Then a new minister arrived. His vision for the youthwork called for a high level of competence on the part of all helpers. The middle-aged man was told he was no longer required. The current state of his self-esteem is far, far worse than the first.

There may be a tension between the opportunity of affirming others in the church by giving them a task to do, and that of achieving a vision. You alone can decide but take care 'that the exercise of your freedom does not become a stumbling-block to the weak' (1 Corinthians 8:9).

The Perspective of Scripture

Two points are included here: the first covers self-esteem; the second, those many other 'self' words.

We looked at the biblical basis of self-esteem earlier in this chapter. Help the person who comes to you to absorb that teaching until it becomes his or her own. It may take some time to move from the head to the heart but persevere.

The other 'self' words have not engaged our attention and therefore deserve a few sentences. Self-denial has featured high on the agenda of evangelicals for a long time. The self which is to be denied is what Irenaeus referred to as 'carnal man'. Contemporary writers such as Heather Ward and Paul Tournier describe it as the ego. It is that unredeemed part of me which seeks satisfaction for its own sake. This is not the Christian way and we should be wary of those approaches which offer personal growth in the shape of self-fulfilment and self-actualization apart from Christ. Many engaged in pastoral counselling and spiritual direction draw heavily on the works of Carl Jung. His writings certainly contain great insights which can be used very effectively, but all must be measured against the touchstone of scripture. The Jungian foundations of identity, espoused by many counsellors and psychotherapists, do not stand the test of biblical investigation.[33] They have to be handled with care, a point made earlier from the writings of Christopher Bryant and Bruce Duncan. Our true selves (or as St Augustine expresses it, our hearts) can only find themselves in God.

The Empowerment of Purposeful Support

Grace Sheppard writes of the enormous fillip given to her self-esteem when another person used the words 'You can do it'.[34] There was a sense of empowerment and liberation which is often lacking amongst those whose self-worth is low. Such empowerment has to focus on the practical and not the theoretical. It must concern itself with realistic goals for finding the right work, paid or unpaid, as in the case of Christine, or finding any work at all, as in the case of Monica's husband and son. As the person offering pastoral care, you may feel as powerless as the one you are seeking to help when it comes to finding work. Others may be far better placed than you, and you will do well to keep an up-to-date list of those others in the shape of government agencies, self-help clubs and the like. But whenever there is a possibility of something – albeit a little something – get alongside the one who needs you and encourage him or her in each step they take on their way.

8

LOSS OF WORK

I have learned the secret of being content in any and every situation ... whether living in plenty or in want.

(Philippians 4:12)

Our attention now turns to the oldest member of the group: Frank, the other churchwarden.

Frank's Story

Frank is in his mid-50s. He is married to Joyce, whom he met at the bank where they both worked. They have two married children, one living in the Midlands and the other who has emigrated to Australia. Joyce was obliged to give up her job when she married Frank, for it was the policy of the bank at that time never to employ married couples. The policy has long since changed but Joyce has never considered returning, having involved herself in a variety of church-based and other activities while the children were growing up, and having continued to do so now that they have left home.

Frank's parents had been delighted that he had got a job in one of the high-street banks when he left school. For them it symbolized security, respectability and responsibility. He had risen slowly, a fact he attributed to the greater ambition of his colleagues and not to their ability. He had been moved on three occasions but only had to move house once to their present home. The family had always attended church and played an active part in church life; for example, Frank has had a long spell as treasurer and is still chairman of the finance committee, as well as being church-warden. He has also been involved in other activities, first on the PTA of the school his children attended and then as a school governor. The bank had encouraged him in this latter position, allowing him a limited amount of time off as part of the organization's community involvement policy.

Frank and Joyce also play bowls, an interest inherited from his father. Many of their friends are members of the bowls club where, predictably enough, Frank continues to serve as a member of the finance and general purposes sub-committee.

He has always been immensely proud of the bank. Memorabilia are discreetly scattered around the house – the carriage clock presented to him on his thirtieth anniversary; a photograph of him shaking hands with the chairman; a framed article from a local newspaper showing him donating a cheque for £5000 to a school for the blind. Such is his pride that he becomes quite aggressive whenever anyone criticizes the bank, revealing an aspect of his personality that surprises all but those who know him well. He had, indeed, become particularly angry on one occasion when Christine, the new curate's wife, had condemned the bank for its criminal irresponsibility (her words) towards third-world countries by making substantial loans and then demanding abnormally high (her words again) levels of interest, plunging a poor country into irretrievable bankruptcy (her final comment). He has seldom spoken to her since then and avoids her whenever possible.

The day when he was called to the manager's office was the worst day in his life. He realized that something was amiss when he entered the office and saw the Regional Personnel Manager sitting there. She, in fact, did most of the talking, outlining the enormous advantages and opportunities of the early retirement package which was being 'offered' to him. He went straight from the meeting to the lavatory and threw up.

Frank has still not got used to his early retirement, despite the fact that several of his friends at the bowls club are in a similar position. At first, he hardly dared to visit them and now goes less frequently than before. Joyce finds it hard to have him around all the time, particularly when he is morose which seems to be a growing feature of his existence.

Despite all the fine phrases like 'early retirement', 'new opportunities' and 'the next stage of your life', Frank knows that he is no longer needed and it hurts him deeply. He has lost his job and, with it, a part – a large part – of himself. Frank is afflicted with that terrible contemporary disease of industrial countries – the disease of being surplus to requirements, of being redundant.

Redundancy

In this chapter we will consider the subject of redundancy and suggest some of the ways that you may offer pastoral care to those who are faced with it.

The very first task I had in the personnel department at Ford Motor Company in Dagenham was to do with redundancy. In that year – 1965 – the Redundancy Payments Act had become law in the UK. This provided some protection for employees who had been laid off and needed to bridge the financial gap in their earnings before they found another job in what was, in most parts of the UK, a state of full employment. Ford had negotiated an agreement with the unions, which was to provide the model adopted by many other companies and which defined a principle for selecting those to be made redundant. The principle was that of LIFOOTBE – last in, first out, other things being equal. The 'other things being equal' clause enabled the company to keep a small number of recent employees whose particular skills were in very short supply, and to maintain their statutory 'quota' of registered disabled employees. At that time, a slump in car sales had led first to a recruitment ban and then to short-time working. The possibility of 'laying off' people (the phrase at the time) was now a reality. My task was to collect details of all leavers on a weekly basis (30,000 people were employed on the Dagenham site), and to adjust the redundancy list in the light of the next month's estimated labour requirements. In the event, a revival in car sales changed the scene entirely and we were soon back to full recruitment mode.

Thirty years ago, redundancy in the UK was rare or, to be more accurate, had been rare since the Second World War. It happened to particular sectors of the workforce – the unskilled – and affected certain parts of the country more than others – the industrial North and the Midlands rather than the South. It did not happen to those employed in banks, insurance companies, schools, the civil service, the armed services and large blue-chip companies. To have been made redundant from a bank or insurance company, for example, was at one and the same time a social stigma and a massive obstacle to re-employment.

All of that has now changed. Redundancy is a common feature of the employment scene. No employment sector has escaped as the managements of organizations have reduced numbers under the joint banners of productivity and profit. It is no longer the social stigma it once was. In some ways, Frank's predicament is less serious than many others. He has worked all his life for one company and is financially secure. Countless others, though, are in a much worse state – younger than Frank, they may have dependants and financial commitments. Although redundancy does not create the barrier to re-employment it once did, it has deeply affected attitudes towards work, and many see little hope for the future. Theirs is a sore affliction. Redundancy, and its companion, unemployment, are scourges almost apocalyptic in their devastation.

Before we focus on the hurt that redundancy still causes, let us remind ourselves of the main causes.

The Causes of Redundancy

I have highlighted five causes which are often closely inter-related. The list is not exhaustive but sufficiently comprehensive for our purpose.

Changes in Working Practices

In recent years, many employers have attempted to become more efficient in the way they use their employees. They have adopted one or more of a number of techniques with similar results, namely, the need for fewer people. Organizations have been restructured and layers of management removed. This was the case with the bank employing Frank which, almost certainly, will also have reduced the number of its high-street outlets. Along with countless others, the bank will have looked at the way its operations are conducted and will have changed them to remove unnecessary transactions. Consultants call this 'business process re-engineering'. In line with lots of big companies, the bank might have contracted out many of the activities previously undertaken by its employees on the grounds that they are not part of the 'core business'; for example, catering, cleaning, data processing and a myriad of other activities will now be conducted by contractors. Unlike many other organizations, it will not have relocated although this, too, is a practice adopted in an attempt to reduce labour costs.

The end result of these fundamental changes in organization – and they are continuing relentlessly – is threefold:

1. Fewer people are required to conduct the work.

2. Some of the tasks previously carried out by full-time employees can now be accomplished by part-timers.

3. Employees at all levels, from the school-leaver to the main board director, are expected to work much harder (see chapter six on stress). This in turn is creating new divisions in society for 'some have work and money but too little time, while others have all the time but no work and no money.'[1]

Changes in Technology

In the period since the Second World War, technological innovation has changed at a bewildering speed. Experiences from my own working life are typical of what has happened over the past 30 years.

When I started with Fords in the early '60s, the assembly lines were manned (the word is correct, for the workforce was entirely male) by thousands of people performing routine tasks, which are now handled by robots controlled by a computer. At my next employer, John Laing, the highly sophisticated mainframe computer was housed in a building of its own, such was its size and its sensitivity to the surrounding atmosphere. The power of that computer is less than that contained in an ordinary PC. When I moved to RTZ in the early '70s, the first portable calculating machines were on the market. They cost the equivalent of four weeks' wages for the average shopfloor worker. The cheapest calculator today is much more powerful and is the same price as two rounds of sandwiches.

The manufacturing organizations which dominated the employment scene of most Western countries are rapidly being replaced by information organizations. The 'chip' is having a similar impact on society to that of the steam engine in the eighteenth century, except that the impact is more rapid and more widely felt.

The impact of these technological changes was foreseen many years ago. Norbert Wiener, the mathematician who contributed so much to the communications revolution and invented the name 'cybernetics' to describe it, foretold the consequences, and highlighted some of the moral dilemmas we would face.[2] But his advice, and that of others like him, was ignored as we eagerly embraced each new advance. The benefits have, of course, been enormous in many instances but the inevitable effect has been that fewer people are required – many jobs previously undertaken by humans are now carried out more speedily and effectively by machines. It is a re-run of the Industrial Revolution, but the change is faster and it is happening everywhere.

Changes in the Market Place

Employers can only provide work if the goods produced, or services offered, are in demand at a price which supports the continued operations of the enterprise. Hundreds of companies have closed down because they could no longer sell their products at a viable price. This is the cause of Monica's husband, Alf, being out of work. The failure of his employer to invest in new machinery and the failure of Alf to develop new skills has meant liquidation for the former and redundancy and unemployment for the latter. Tom faces a similar problem. In his case it is not a failure to invest – he has done that. It is that his share of the market has decreased such that he has no choice but to reduce his workforce.

One of the features of the past 20 years that has contributed to this market change is international competition. Domestic and export markets are now inextricably bound together. Competition used to come predominantly from the factory in the next town. Now it comes from factories across the world.

Changes in Government Policy

Government policy has been the direct or indirect cause of many redundancies over the past decade and a half. This is the case in the UK and may be true of other countries – I cannot comment knowledgeably on the latter. Three particular aspects of policy contribute to the loss of jobs. The first is the reduction in public spending. Cutting expenditure on roads and housing, for example, cripples the construction companies and puts many out of work. Decisions of this sort are political, born of fiscal policies and dogma. They may be essential, but the consequences are clear for all to see: fewer people than before are needed.

The second is privatization. Regardless of the arguments for and against privatization, two outcomes are always predictable. The first is that the numbers employed have been reduced significantly with employees from all levels being made redundant. The second is that the earning structure has changed markedly with those at the top multiplying their income many times over and those at the bottom frequently being asked to take a cut in the interests of competitive demands.

The third is accountability. Schools, universities, hospitals, indeed, the whole sphere of education and health, have been forced to restructure to satisfy the principles of political dogma. The results have been an increase in administrative and managerial staff and a massive reduction in the numbers of teachers, nurses and other professionals.

Changes in Ownership

Every so often, 'merger mania' infects business. It happens far more in the US and the UK than in Europe and the Far East, where the structures of capitalism are different from the English-speaking countries. Some of the mergers make obvious sense but many bear the hallmark of greed. It is well known that a majority of mergers fail, but the practice continues and will undoubtedly do so as long as shareholders look for a short-term return on their investments. There is, however, one certain outcome of any merger: the numbers employed by the merged companies will be fewer than the numbers employed by each of the separate companies.

The Practice of Making People Redundant

Redundancy seems inevitable for the foreseeable future, certainly in the older industrialized countries who are constantly cutting their cost base to compete with the more recently arrived players. Lawyers talk about jobs being made redundant. The reality is that people, not jobs, are made redundant. In the UK, the law of the land dictates minimum standards to be followed when redundancies are declared and government guidelines encourage good practice over and above those minima. In most countries of the European Union, the law protects the employee more than in the UK. The reverse is true in the USA. It may be of use to you in your pastoral caring role to know what is seen as constituting good practice and this is briefly summarized below. If any who read this book are in a position to influence the organization in which they work to adopt good practice, I urge them to do so. It is part of our prophetic role as Christians to see that justice prevails.

Precautionary Action

When it becomes clear to an employer that, for one or more of the reasons mentioned above, there are likely to be too many people for the work to be done, the first action to be taken is a ban on hiring. This should be accompanied by an investigation of the various alternatives, including short-time working, extended holidays, etc.

Giving Warning

If, despite this action and investigation, redundancy appears the only solution to the business problem, as much warning as possible should be given to those likely to be involved. This is a practice not widely used, with many employers resorting to the statutory minimum or ignoring it altogether. A recent change in UK law has addressed this and brought us into line with other European countries requiring consultation with all concerned.

Selecting Those Affected

The selection of those to be made redundant has to be demonstrably fair. This either means that it complies with a procedure already defined and communicated by the employer, or with generally accepted criteria, such as 'last in first out'. Many companies, as in Frank's case, encourage people to take early retirement, but this is a diminishing option as there are fewer older employees to whom this opportunity can now be made. Moreover, it is extremely expensive.

Breaking the News

Then comes the task of giving each person an early warning, together with an undertaking to search for alternative employment within the organization – a search which rarely succeeds. This advance notice should be followed with a letter setting out the terms, which must not be less than the statutory minima and frequently are not more. Notice should never be given on the day before a weekend or a public holiday, for it leaves the person powerless to do anything other than immerse his or her family and friends in the problem.

Providing Support

Psychological support is needed on two fronts. The person giving the news needs to understand the range of likely reactions which may take place. The person receiving the news should know immediately where they can turn for information, guidance and help.

Practical support is also needed. Good practice includes helping employees with the search for new employment and allowing them time off and the use of facilities (for example, telephone, photocopiers, etc.) as they pursue their quest. Some organizations go further still and engage external consultants to provide professional help in the job search.

So much for good practice. Regrettably, it is honoured as much, perhaps more, in the breach than in the observance. All too many people are told to leave on the day they receive the news, giving them no opportunity to say goodbye to colleagues and scarcely enough time to clear their locker or desk.

The impact of redundancy, as we shall shortly see, is painful no matter how well it is handled. The added pain caused by bad handling can do incalculable harm to a person's sense of self-worth.

The Impact of Redundancy on the Person

An earlier book in this series[3] included redundancy among other major losses which many of us experience in the course of our life. The reactions of someone being made redundant often follow a similar pattern to those of bereavement. Let us, then, look at this pattern as an aid to our understanding in our role of pastoral care, bearing in mind that it is a typical pattern and not a universal process that everyone does or must experience.[4]

Shock

No matter how widely the word has spread on the forthcoming redundancies, there is still a sense of shock when the person is told. Up until that moment there is always the possibility that the axe will fall on someone else. In some ways, it is akin to the shock of a bereavement except that it is happening to the person concerned and not a relative or a friend. The numbness which can accompany shock is frequently experienced and it is therefore unwise for the person delivering the news – who is seen as some kind of executioner – to spend too much time explaining the background and the consequences. This is best left to another person or to a later meeting.

Shock is likely to have a different effect on those who have anticipated the event emotionally, in contrast to those who have only considered it intellectually. The former may experience less shock than the latter.

Relief

This is a common reaction, particularly when the reality of redundancy has been publicized either formally or via the grapevine. I well remember an ex-colleague telling me that he felt so much better when he knew he was being made redundant than when he thought he might be. Certainty gives rise to relief.

Disbelief

Although some experience relief, others do not believe the news to be true. There must be some mistake ... it is all some sort of nightmare. This is usually a brief phase, for the reality is easily tested. If it persists it can cause serious problems.

Denial

Denial is a natural and, in many ways, healthy reaction. It is close to disbelief except that it does not allow for the possibility of reality. It can take three forms. There are those who continue to work as though nothing has happened. They report at starting time and leave with their colleagues seven or eight hours later. Such people will be assiduous in their work, wanting to ensure that everything is in good working order. They often have to be faced with the fact that their time with the employer is fast running out and that they should plan future action.

Another reaction takes the form of adopting the old work pattern, but not going to work. This is a not infrequent response, particularly among those who commute regularly into a large city. It is easy to maintain a show of working whilst spending each day engaged in meaningless activity. Such people recognize the reality for themselves but hide it from their spouse, their children and their neighbours.

A third common form of denial is the denial of any negative feelings. This can result in serious problems once a new job has been found and the person feels safe in their employment. Sometimes, the stored-up anger and depression force their way to the surface and are totally inexplicable to the person concerned. This becomes the 'pathological grief' which can produce mental illness and worse.[5]

Anger

Most people experience this. It may be directed against the employer or against the person who has conveyed the message; it may turn to intense hatred for a while. 'I wanted to kill you for about three days after you had told me,' said someone whom I had made redundant, 'but that has now all gone.' For some it takes much longer than others. One such had managed a design department for some years and was suddenly declared redundant. I saw him for counselling when the presenting problem was stress, manifesting itself in verbal abuse towards his family and neighbours. As we met over several weeks, he told me of the intense anger he felt towards his ex-employer. He had thought seriously of buying a gun; he had driven his car past the building hoping he might see his ex-boss and run him down. The feelings he expressed when redundancy happened were as great, if not greater, eighteen months later. It took another three or four months for him to deal effectively with his anger.

Christians can find it difficult to express their anger which, in this context, is intrinsically good. Repressed anger, like any other strong emotion, finds an outlet in later years – often in depression or uncontrolled outbursts of temper.

This raises an important point. Some of the reactions to redundancy, as in the case of a bereavement, may be shortlived but for others they may last a long time. The pattern for each person is unique.

A Loss of Self-Esteem

In the previous chapter we saw how work can provide people with a sense of self and a feeling of self-esteem. Frank is an all too typical example. The concept of self-worth is hard hit by redundancy, no matter what the cause of it. Even when it has been brought about by the relocation of a factory or an office to another country, people may still experience a massive reduction in their own self-esteem. 'I will have to prove myself all over again' was the embittered reaction of one extremely capable person who lacked any positive feelings of self-worth.

A Feeling of Isolation

In a relatively short time, the busy worker surrounded by colleagues and engaged in familiar tasks has become, as he or she often sees it, just another statistic on the unemployment register. In the early stages, the fact that many have travelled along a similar route is of little comfort because each individual rightly believes themselves to be unique, but wrongly to be utterly isolated. Such people will find it impossible, or very painful, to return to their erstwhile place of work, to collect belongings or documents. This feeling is often exacerbated by the embarrassment felt by those colleagues still at work who do not know how to deal with their one-time companion. They also see themselves as outsiders and this feeling may affect their contacts with other non-work colleagues. Frank, it will be recalled, found it hard at first to show up at the bowls club.

Mental and Physical Distress

The symptoms associated with stress which we noted in an earlier chapter are often apparent here. They include anxiety, which is frequently associated with one's financial situation; depression, as people can see themselves in a prison from which they cannot escape; and lethargy, as they do not know how to summon up the energy required to engage in the job search.

We must never underestimate the strength of these feelings, avoiding the sort of well-intentioned Christian responses which cause so much damage. People faced with a severe financial crisis are seldom helped by being assured that 'the Lord will provide'. And those with few marketable skills in an area of high unemployment are not necessarily encouraged by being told to regard their loss as an opportunity. But more of this later. If the grief is well handled, the next stage is likely to be more positive.

Acceptance

As in bereavement, or in any other major loss, the final stage is that where the person fully accepts the reality of the situation and begins the next stage of his or her journey. For some this may happen quickly, for others it can take months, for still others it may never take place. Monica's husband, Alf, seems to be unable to break out of his negative state, which is a very serious one since it has lasted five years. Frank, too, is having real problems despite a satisfactory financial settlement and a lot of activities in which he can engage.

Strategies for Pastoral Care

How can we help the likes of Frank and Alf to face up to and work through their loss? The strategies listed below are often sequential but not necessarily so. In this, and in all other aspects of pastoral care, the starting point is to recognize and, where necessary, affirm individual differences. Choose, then, from these approaches those which seem most appropriate to you as you listen to, and come to understand, the person's unique story.

Allow Time to Grieve

Job's three friends sat with him in silence for seven days when they visited him at the time of his loss (Job 2:13). Theirs was the 'compassion of a silent presence'.[6] It is easy to overlook the importance of grieving following redundancy because of the need to engage in the job search. Substituting grieving with action can have long-term negative effects on a person's well-being, which are much more difficult to address. Share their suffering and grief in so far as you are able. By bearing each other's burdens we fulfil the law of Christ (Galatians 6:2).

Encourage the Expression of Emotions

These might be many and varied. Anger is very common. Consider using the imprecatory psalms[7] as one way of expressing anger. Shouting one or more of these can provide a release of emotions at least as effective as the psychotherapist's pillow. Sadness is another common emotion. Men such as Frank, who are in their 50s, are not accustomed to shed tears. Help them to cry, for it has enormous therapeutic value. Yet another healing aid comes from the reassurance you can give that the emotions being expressed are normal. The emotions will vary in intensity but the realization that others have shared them can be of great comfort.

There may also be some unfinished business to attend to by the person. Redundancy, particularly when handled badly and in a hurry, does not encourage the fitting ending most of us would expect. You cannot force an unwilling person, but you can encourage them to address these necessary endings. They might be able to handle them in a way which recovers their dignity. An ex-client of mine is a case in point. He was very embittered by redundancy and took many months to find a new job. Concerned about his strong feelings, he was encouraged to arrange a celebration party to which he invited some of his old workmates, including the person who had delivered the message and about whom he had raged so often. The celebration was well attended, allowed reconciliation between him and his ex-boss and enabled him to start anew in a healthy mental state.

Aim to be Realistic and Avoid Platitudes

In order to be effective in coming to terms with the dismissal and seeking a new job, you have to get the person grounded in reality. Do it sensitively and not brutally. Simple direct phrases such as 'You have lost your job and you need to find a new one' focus the mind much more effectively than an effusion of language. Remember that the person is more vulnerable than usual so avoid any statements which may be interpreted as casting doubt on that person's faith or spiritual well-being.

A Christian friend, greatly experienced in helping people to handle redundancy and find new work, talks of the three phases or tasks of out-placement. They are:

- dealing with unfinished business: practical, financial and emotional
- considering options and choosing a direction
- implementing the job search.

I have dwelt on the first, emphasizing the importance of giving adequate time to the process. Help with the second can be found in chapter five on vocation. I will add a few words here to supplement those earlier remarks on job choice and deal at the same time with the third phase.

Give Practical Assistance

Negotiating the emotional rocks is a vital step but only one step. Others of a more practical sort have to be taken which may occur at

the same time, or separately. There are no rules, but here are a few
fundamental points:

Encourage Self-Discipline

The pattern of work having been disrupted, it is all too easy to slide
into an unstructured, meaningless way of life. Help the person to
develop a new pattern within which they pursue their job search.
Encourage them to improve their mental, physical and spiritual well-
being for these can have a positive effect on the job search.

Identify Support Mechanisms

These may be within or outside the Church, though the former can
have a special impact when openness, informed sharing and prayer
are part of the local church's lifestyle. For some, the eucharistic
symbols of the broken bread and shed blood can be a major support.
Consider introducing a communion service on a regular basis for
those without work.

Refer to Others for Help

Finding a new job is a full-time activity. That neat statement summa-
rizes the experience of many people. Some people who have been
made redundant are given help by out-placement or career counsellors to assist them in finding their new work. The majority are not.
Be ready with the list you have drawn up in connection with finding
suitable employment (see chapter five), and refer them to people
who can help or manuals of self-help.

Rekindle Self-Esteem

Having covered this in the previous chapter, I recommend you to
revisit the strategies set out there.

Discover God in the Situation

Using scripture for meditation has been of immense value to some, I
know, but be careful not to impose particular passages. Reflecting on
the sufferings of Christ may not be helpful to those who can see no
resurrection and have no sense of having completed their work. Ask

them to tell you of passages that are, or have been, important to them and help them to use these as the basis for their reflection. If they want more guidance on this, a helpful book is that by Peter Curran which contains 30 daily readings and meditations.[8]

The Celtic Church honoured three martyrdoms. The red martyrdom was that of giving one's life for Christ, of dying for the faith. The green martyrdom was the daily practice of self-denial, so as to grow more like Christ. The white martyrdom was the way of exile, of Christian men and women leaving their homes to follow God's leading. The Christian faith of many Europeans resulted from those who adopted the white martyrdom. Writing of the Celtic tradition, Esther de Waal likens white martyrdom in the Western world to

> *the loss of place within society, through unemployment and early retirement ... of not belonging anywhere.*[9]

Our Christian ancestors found asceticism a source of profound spiritual growth. For the right person – but certainly not for all – this thought may be a seed to sow at the proper time.

Structure an Appropriate Lifestyle

We started with Frank and will finish with him. His predicament is different from younger men and women who are without work, and wish and need to get back into it. Many of the strategies set out above can be put to use in his case but, perhaps, the most important one is that of creating a new way of living and working. You can help him with his negative emotions and his loss of self-esteem. You can introduce him to a new structure which integrates his activities and his devotions. An adaptation of the Benedictine Rule might be very valuable to someone with Frank's experience. You can also help him emotionally by relocating his experience in an appropriate place. For the most part, Frank's experience at the bank was one of great satisfaction. This has been soured by the events of the past few months of employment. Encourage him to reminisce about the good times and, as he does so, help him to separate them from the brief, unpleasant ones. Then help him to put the whole experience into some sort of perspective. Get him to illustrate his experience or to write about it. You may well find that once he knows how to recall these positive experiences, he can use them whenever he likes and begin to build a whole new life for himself and his wife.

9

WOMEN AND WORK

... a woman who fears the Lord is to be praised.
Give her the reward she has earned.
                    (Proverbs 31:30, 31)

The next person we meet is Sally, close friend of Christine and everyone's helper.

Sally's Story

Sally is in her early 30s and has two small children. She is married to Doug, the manager of one of the out-of-town supermarkets in the area. Sally had been employed as a secretary/PA before the birth of her first child who is now in her second year at infant school. Her son is 18 months younger than his sister and attends nursery school three mornings a week. Her husband, Doug, is the youth leader in the church and tackles it with the energetic enthusiasm he devotes to every activity he undertakes. An adherent of the charismatic renewal movement for some time, he persuaded Peter about a year ago to restructure the Sunday evening worship so as to appeal to young people. This has been extremely successful with the youth in the area and now boasts its own rock band which has twice been invited to other churches.

Sally is wholly supportive of Doug's work with the young people, although she does not entirely share his single-minded enthusiasm. She enjoys the comings and goings of the teenagers, and her two children love the attention heaped on them by the constant flow of visitors.

Sally and Doug are struggling to make ends meet and Sally can see the financial demands steadily increasing as the children get older. Soon after the younger child started nursery school, therefore, she raised the possibility of doing some 'temping' on a limited-hours basis.

Doug dismissed the suggestion out of hand. He reiterated his strongly held view that a young mother's place is in the home and that God will provide. Sally agreed in principle but pointed out that she could fit in the work while the children were at school, thereby being available for them whenever they needed her. Doug was adamant and she has not felt able to raise the subject again.

Not long after the conversation, however, Sally was distressed to discover that, without consulting her, Doug had mentioned to Peter, the vicar, and James, his curate, that she had spare time available which could be put to good use at the church. Since then she has been bombarded – or so it feels – with requests to undertake a range of tedious administrative tasks for both vicar and curate. She has acceded to all their requests with a smiling face and a sinking heart. Sally feels as though she is at everyone's beck and call: the children; Doug; the teenagers from the youth group; the vicar; the curate; the list is endless, yet she never gets any thanks. She is taken for granted and is constantly being given new tasks to carry out, for which she feels less and less enthusiasm. And all of this, she hears others say, is for God. She wants to scream at God but his response, she feels sure, will be a holier, grander version of Doug's. She feels trapped and altogether worthless.

A Woman's Place

Sally is struggling with a problem which is having a negative impact on her relationships with family and friends. It also affects her walk with God. She feels that what she does is of little or no value. She is not alone in this feeling. Western society ascribes great value to money. It is, as it claims, a capitalist society. We are the inheritors, or perhaps the victims, of what Thomas Carlyle disparagingly called the 'cash nexus' – the concept that all transactions, including human ones, can be measured in financial terms.

Work is a prime example of this. Work for which a payment is made is perceived as more important than work where it is not. This is well illustrated by the introduction 'I am only a housewife' used by extremely capable women, who do an incredibly important job yet apologize for their existence. Note, in particular, the emphasis of the statement on the identity of the person in contrast to the activity it involves. It suggests that 'being' a housewife is of lesser value than 'being' a shop assistant, a policeman or a double glazing salesman. It confuses identity with role.

In this chapter we will consider work for which no payment is made and the aspects of pastoral care associated with it. The chapter focuses on women, especially women with young children, and covers three work themes:

Work where the need is determined by the family: this includes looking after children and caring for dependants who are incapable of caring for themselves; the latter embraces those with a physical or mental handicap, those who are sick and those whose age has restricted their coping skills.

Work which involves serving others in a voluntary capacity: this is an enormously varied field, including Sally's many church-related activities and Monica's involvement with Guides. No church can exist without such people.

Work in which a wife and mother combines the two roles listed above with employment work: this is a growing practice in developed countries.

The pastoral care we offer in each or all of these circumstances is affected by our views on the role of women in the home, the Church and employment. This will constitute our starting point.

The Influence of Feminism

No debate on this subject can ignore the feminist movement. In its current form, it is a post-Second World War phenomenon, with a major landmark being the publication of Simone de Beauvoir's *The Second Sex*[1] in 1949. Feminist theology has been greatly influenced by feminism and started in earnest about 20 years later with the publication in 1968 of Mary Daly's book *The Church and the Second Sex*.[2] It has since given birth to many books, some of which are referred to in this chapter.

The issues arising from feminism have taken on substantial proportions in the field of secular employment since the composition of the workforce has changed so fundamentally. In developed countries, there are now as many women as men employed although a majority of the women are in part-time and, for the most part, lower-paid occupations. The Christian Church's response to feminism has been varied but seldom indifferent. Some have seen it as a passing fashion; others as a pernicious influence to be resisted; still others as a liberating force for women and men alike.[3] Within the Anglican Church, the subject matter came to a head in the UK with the 1992 debate on the ordination of women to the priesthood. During that debate the Archbishop of Canterbury declared that 'There is no connection between the ordination of women to the priesthood and feminism',[4] although many others have found it extremely difficult to disentangle the two.[5]

At the root of the feminist campaign is the principle of equality, a principle on which the Bible is clear. Therefore, we will start with the scriptures, in order to inform our views on the woman's role in the home, Church and workplace.

The Biblical View of Equality

Equal in God's Sight

Long before the current debate began, Dorothy L. Sayers commented:

> *The question of sex-equality is, like all questions affecting human relationships, delicate and complicated.*[6]

The comment was made in the early part of an address given in 1938 and provocatively titled 'Are women human?'. The substance of her argument was that women are indeed human and should be treated like other human beings who have thoughts, opinions, skills and all that contributes to being human. This right to similar treatment, she argued, derives from their humanity, not their sexuality.

The Bible – and Dorothy L. Sayers being both a Christian and a scholar uses the Bible to support her case – certainly affirms the equality between men and women.

> *Then God said, 'Let us make man in our image, in our likeness, and let them rule over the fish of the sea and the birds of the air, over the livestock, over all the earth, and over all the creatures that move along the ground.'*
>
> *So God created man in his own image.*
> *In the image of God he created him;*
> *Male and female he created them.* (Genesis 1:26, 27)

We have already explored the meaning of the word 'image' in chapter two and we will not repeat here what we said there. An additional facet, which is of particular pertinence in our present context, is that the reflection of God's image in male and female suggests an androgynous quality in the Godhead, a union of all that is masculine and feminine. So avers John Stott, commenting that

> *There must be within the being of God ... something which corresponds to the 'feminine' as well as the 'masculine' in humankind.*[7]

This certainly makes sense when we take seriously the female and maternal metaphors of God in the Bible (for example, Deuteronomy 32:8; Isaiah 49:15),[8] although it does not undermine the emphasis of scripture that the essential relationship with the Divine is that of father and child. This equality is changed by the Fall. Adam now exercises dominion over the woman, demonstrating that dominion by the authoritative act of naming her Eve. Yet the equality is restored by Christ's redemptive work:

> *There is neither Jew nor Greek, slave nor free, male nor female, for you are all one in Christ Jesus.* (Galatians 3:28)

And so we see that in the relationships of the sexes, as in work, the original plan of creation is once more made good by Christ's work of redemption.

Equal but Different

Men and women are equal, yet clearly men and women are different. They are united in their humanity but distinct in their sexuality. The biblical view is that of complementarity, a state designed by God but, as with work, distorted by the Fall. The second creation account contains the following:

> *But for Adam [i.e. man] no suitable helper was found so the Lord God caused the man to fall into a deep sleep and while he was sleeping, he took one of the man's ribs and closed up the place with flesh. Then the Lord God made a woman from the rib he had taken out of the man and he brought her to the*

man. The man said 'This is now bone of my bones and flesh of my flesh; she shall be called woman, for she was taken out of man.' (Genesis 2:20–3)

The interpretations given to these verses have been many and varied. Living at the end of the twentieth century, the picture conjured up is one of surgery under anaesthetic, but such a practice was unknown to the author of Genesis and must be dismissed as a possible interpretation. The only conclusion we can draw is that we have here a glimpse of a mystery, but that it remains – and will remain – a mystery.

There is, though, one aspect in this passage which we must dwell on because it affects the role of women. It is that of the meaning of 'helper' in verses 18 and 20. The Hebrew word is 'ezer' which is used 21 times in the Old Testament. Of these, the word is used on 15 occasions to refer to God (for example, Psalm 124:8; Deuteronomy 33:7), from which we can conclude that a helper is frequently someone with superior power rather than someone in an inferior position. In this Genesis passage, however, the word does not signify status but role, and the role here is one of complementarity rather than subordination. The word 'suitable' used in the NIV is anodyne, as is the RSV's 'fit'. Far better is the AV's 'meet' (meaning 'appropriate') or the NEB's use of 'partner'.

Women and men in the creation account have a complementary role, a mutual partnership. Matthew Henry captures it succinctly in what, nearly 300 years later, seems to us a quaint manner. Woman was

> *not made out of his [man's] head to top him, not out of his feet to be trampled upon by him, but out of his side to be equal with him, under his arm to be protected, and near his heart to be beloved.*[9]

This was the situation before the Fall. But with the Fall the situation changed. Domination entered and the so-called battle between the sexes began.

To the woman he [God] said: 'I will greatly increase your pains in child-birth; with pain you will give birth to children. Your desire will be for your husband, and he will rule over you.' (Genesis 3:16)

The mutual partnership ordained by God is replaced by 'instinctive urges, passive and active'.[10] Relationships between the sexes can still be beautiful and fulfilling, as can childbearing and work, but the situation now is one where sin is 'forever crouching at the door' (Genesis 4:7).

The Role of Women in Marriage and in the Home

There are two common situations we encounter today. One arises where the woman carries out the work of a housewife and home-based mother. The other is where the woman arranges for that work to be done, wholly or in part, by one or more others – be they the husband, relatives, neighbours or paid help.

The fundamental issue to be addressed is the biblical teaching of the role of women and men in marriage. There are conflicting views held by evangelicals on this, as well as on the related themes of the woman's role in Church and at work.[11] The debate revolves around the meaning of 'headship', a word used by Elaine Storkey, Leanne Payne and others[12] to describe the relationship between husband and wife portrayed in the New Testament. Although not all agree with his conclusion, I find John Stott's assertion compelling: that the New Testament teaches man's headship as deriving from the priority of creation (i.e. man was created before woman), the mode of creation (i.e. woman was created from man) and the purpose of creation (i.e. woman was created for man).[13] But this headship was not intended by God to be of the autocratic, domineering kind. That so-called headship was the result of the Fall and is roundly criticized in the New Testament, though frequently practised by Christian men, past and present. The headship of the husband in marriage is based on two analogies. The first is the headship of God in relation to Christ; the second the headship of Christ in relation to the Church. Both of these are included in Paul's first letter to the Corinthians:

...The head of every man is Christ, and the head of the woman is man, and the head of Christ is God. (11:3)

Here we see a hierarchy of 'originating and subordinating' relationships of God, Christ, man and woman.[14] The nature of this relationship is clarified when we concentrate on the second of the analogies, namely, that of Christ in relation to the Church. From Ephesians 5 we learn that Paul makes 'the union between Christ and the Church, the prototype for the relationship of believing husbands and wives'.[15]

This relationship calls for voluntary submission on the part of wives to their husbands, on the grounds that 'The husband is the head of the wife as Christ is head of the Church, his body, of which he is the saviour' (Ephesians 5:23). This submission – and the word clearly denotes authority on the part of the other person – calls for a response from husbands, once again based on Christ's relationship with the Church:

Husbands love your wives, just as Christ loved the Church and gave himself up for her to make her holy. (Ephesians 5:25, 26a)

The headship of the Christian husband, therefore, is to be modelled on the headship of Christ which is that of loving, self-giving service. 'Applied to marriage,' writes David Field, 'a Christian husband fills the role of "head" most ably when he serves his wife most selflessly.'[16]

The Bible's view of marriage is unequivocal. The husband is the head of the wife. But nowhere does scripture state that a woman's place is in the home. This is a comparatively recent view and not one sanctioned by scripture; even if it were, we would have to make a proper allowance for the fundamental difference between work in the home in biblical times, and work in the home in industrial societies at the end of the twentieth century. Reflect for a moment on the wife's role described in Proverbs 31. She certainly undertakes some of those tasks which later generations have described as 'women's work' – sewing, weaving, cooking and housekeeping, for example, but she does many others which today we would associate with the liberated woman, such as buying and selling property, trading and merchandizing. She also finds time to care for the poor and needy and give wise instruction to others. Many of these activities are no longer home based, for modern civilization

> *has taken all these pleasant and profitable activities out of the home, where the woman looked after them, and handed them over to big industry, to be directed and organized by men at the head of large factories.*[17]

The Role of Women in the Church

The disagreement between evangelicals over relationships between women and men is magnified when it comes to the role of women in the Church, particularly on the subject of ordination. It does not serve our purpose to rehearse the arguments here, which largely revolve around the interpretation of 1 Timothy 2:8–15 and 1 Corinthians 14:33–36, and focus on the meaning of headship and submission in the Ephesian and Corinthian letters we have already noted.[18] In the context of this book it is assumed that women have a whole range of ministries to perform within the Church which are specifically sanctioned by scripture. They include the role of prophet (Acts 21:9; 1 Corinthians 11:5), apostles (Romans 16:7), deacons (Romans 16:1–2) and many others. Most churches would cease to exist without the exercise of these and countless other ministries by thousands of women.

Women and Paid Work

Perhaps the greatest social revolution in Western society in the second half of the twentieth century is the change in the composition of the workforce. Whereas it was once predominantly male, with any females mainly being single, now its composition is roughly equal, with married women as well represented as single women. This trend, it is suggested by those who make a practice of predicting the future, is likely to continue. The change has come about as a result of two influences: one ideological, the other pragmatic. The first is the campaign for equal opportunity in employment; the second is the demographic change brought about by the substantial reduction in birthrates in most Western societies. The realization that this reduction would result in a marked shortage in appropriately skilled people led governments and employers in the 1980s to launch a variety of 'family friendly' policies, as they are generally known. The unforeseen recession in the '90s significantly decelerated the implementation of these policies and brought into question the sincerity of some of the high-flown phrases surrounding equal opportunity.

As well as these major influences, there have been other factors resulting in many more women in paid employment than at any other time except for the two World Wars.

Opportunity

With the notable exception of ordination in the Roman Catholic and Orthodox Churches, and episcopal office in the Church of England, virtually all jobs in most Western countries are now open to women. It is unlawful for employers to discriminate on grounds of sex or marital status in respect of recruitment, promotion, pay and a whole host of other employment practices. The increase in flexibility offered by some employers increases the opportunities available. So, too, does the help given to look after children in the shape of crèches or childcare vouchers which are made available to some women in employment.

Financial Incentives

Many women work in paid employment for survival purposes. They may be a single parent or the wife of an unemployed husband. Monica is one such woman. Either way, they have no choice if they and their family are to eat, drink and be clothed. For some women, the financial incentives are less to do with survival, and more to do with keeping up a preferred lifestyle. This can range from the young couple who are unable to service the mortgage on the property they have purchased unless both have regular incomes (there is a hint of this in the case of Sally and Christine), to those – men as well as women – who wish to enjoy the second car, the extra holiday and the smart clothes.

Career

The opportunities now available to women demand a commitment which allows few deviations. Many return to work after childbirth so that they do not lose out in the career race. Staying at home for such people is seen as a penalty.

Responsibility

There are those who have been trained in a particular sphere who believe they have a duty to use that expertise for the benefit of others. Christine is a good illustration here.

Satisfaction

Women who have time on their hands because the children are at school will wish to use it purposefully. The home-based activities of our mothers and grandmothers, which engaged so much of their attention and energy, have been transformed by labour saving devices. Many look outside the home to find the appropriate outlets for their talents. 'Every woman is a human being,' comments Dorothy L. Sayers, 'and a human being must have occupation, if he or she is not to become a nuisance to the world.'[19]

Equality: Reality or Myth?

Despite massive changes, there is still considerable discrimination at work. Policies exist but practice limps some way behind. Contributing to the Scottish Churches' Industrial Mission Report on Women and Work, Kathy Galloway quotes from United Nations' statistics:

> *Half the world's population is female, two-thirds of the world's work is done by women. They own one-tenth of the world's wealth and one-hundredth of the world's land.*[20]

In industrial countries, three characteristics are obvious:

1. A majority of lowly paid jobs are held by women. This includes professions such as nursing and teaching which demand a level of education as great, if not greater, than that of business which, on the whole, pays very much higher.

2. There are fewer women in senior positions than men. The barrier to promotion, known as the 'glass ceiling', is broken by very few, usually in the most exceptional circumstances and at a cost to their personal life much greater than that of their male colleagues. To get to the top of any enterprise, a woman still has to be far better than her male counterpart.

3. In the increasing number of cases where both husband and wife work, most housework is still done by women. The 'new man' of the '70s and '80s is largely a figment of the imagination, featuring more in TV sitcoms than in reality.

A Christian Perspective

From what we have discussed in this chapter and in other chapters, we can now make five assertions about women and work which will assist us in our pastoral care.

The Fundamental Importance of a Mother's Work

Although the concept of the family differs from nation to nation – for example, the Western nuclear family and the African extended family – in virtually all societies, ancient and modern, it has been the practice for the woman who has borne the child to be the one who spends most time with the child in his or her early years. We see it in the Bible (for example, Hannah and Samuel, Mary and Jesus), and most of us have experienced it in our own lives. The exceptions include the very rich, who delegate the role to a surrogate, and the very poor, who share the task with a relative or neighbour while they go out to earn money for survival. In my view, the work of mothering is the greatest example of human work, reflecting the Divine in its threefold characterization of creation, sustaining and redemption. It is why, instinctively, so many women decide not to return to paid employment in the early years of a child's life, because paid employment can never match the importance of mothering young children in terms of responsibility, influence and complexity.

The influence of the mother on the child in its early years has a profound effect. This is a view shared by most Christians, as well as those who have made it the focus of their research and developmental theories.[21] And although some argue that these writers are all male – and, therefore, biased by definition – their arguments are unconvincing and not shared by women engaged on similar work.[22]

A Woman's Place is not Exclusively in the Home

Having asserted the importance of the mother being with the child in its early years, we would be wrong to extrapolate this view and insist that the woman should *always* remain in the home. For many, it is not a practical alternative since the financial demands on many women are such that they need an income in order to survive. For those who do have a choice, however, there is no biblical teaching which insists on the wife staying at home while the husband goes out to fulfil his task of breadwinner. There are, indeed, many other features which will influence a woman's choice (see chapter five on calling). The choice is in no way limited or proscribed by scriptural injunction.

The Work of the Housewife is of Great Value

The influence for good of the woman who chooses to devote her time and energies to the home can be inestimable. As well as caring for her family, she can discharge two roles beyond the scope of the woman who has employment work away from the home. First, she can carry out the role of the neighbour welcoming others to share her time and possessions. This, as we shall see in the next chapter, is one of the models of pastoral care which can be of substantial value. Second, she can carry out the role of evangelist, demonstrating by her loving acceptance of all others the very nature of Christ's love for humankind.

A Woman's Nature does not Exclude her from Certain Jobs

Are women, by nature, fitted for certain jobs and not others? This is a vexed question for which the answer 'yes' or 'no' has to be qualified immediately by the word 'but'. There are two points which need emphasis:

First women are physically and sexually different from men, a statement which needs no additional evidence to substantiate it! For the most part, women are weaker than men, an adjective used by Peter in his first letter (3:7) referring to 'physical strength, not to intellectual powers, moral courage or spiritual standards'.[23] Apart, then, from the uniquely female work of giving birth to a child, the only work for which women might be less fitted than men is that requiring a degree of strength normally absent from them. Such jobs in industrialized societies now scarcely exist, on account of technological change and health and safety legislation covering the lifting of heavy weights, for example.

Second, the non-physical attributes – variously designated as feminine and masculine – are not exclusive to women and men. The greatest contribution to our thinking on this subject comes from Carl Jung who wrote extensively on what he called the 'anima' and 'animus'. His view was that the unconscious of the male contains a feminine element and the unconscious of the female a masculine one. The preponderance of the anima in women and animus in men is influenced by a variety of factors, among them social conditioning. Jung, however, would not have supported the argument that it is only social conditioning that has influence, for he believed that nature, as well as nurture, were equally important influences which needed to be held in balance. Indeed, it is when women draw heavily on the animus to compete with men that

> they often depreciate or forget those feminine qualities which are equally valuable and absolutely necessary to a balanced and healthy life.[24]

This mixture of the feminine and masculine attributes is, as seen above, the characteristic of God himself which is mirrored in human beings, a point developed in another volume in this series.[25] It follows, therefore, that to classify certain jobs as more suitable to women than to men is to deny the mixture of qualities which exists in male and female, and which makes 'non-anatomical differences ... extraordinarily elusive to demonstrate and define'.[26]

Women may be and, indeed, undoubtedly are in many instances attracted to and better at nursing than men. But there are excellent male nurses who exhibit the same personal qualities as those found in their female counterparts. The exaggerated attention given to the macho image in many employment situations results in a one-dimensional picture of man, which is a perversion of the multi-faceted nature which has been created in the image of God. As a generalization, men might be suited to certain tasks more than women, and vice versa, but to exclude either from the opportunity to tackle any work is not a biblical precept.

All Work, Paid or Unpaid, can have the Same Intrinsic Value

Service in work is a practice to be adopted by all Christians – men and women alike.

The view that women's nature prepares them for service is a dangerous one for two reasons. It suggests, in the first place, that there exists between every man and every woman a cluster of psychological differences – this is demonstrably untrue. Secondly, it distorts the meaning of Christian service. This is a powerful point made by Anne Borrowdale in her book *A Woman's Work*,[27] who argues passionately for a recovery of the Christian ideal of service. She asserts, justifiably, that employers and clergy alike have taken advantage of women by giving them tasks to do which are usually lowly paid on the one hand, and often of little intrinsic value on the other. The basis for such task delegation is that it is a woman's natural inclination to serve.

A truly Christian approach, Borrowdale argues, is that service should be a feature of *all* Christians at work, since this follows the example of Christ the servant, and reinforces the biblical calling to service. Failure to grasp and to practise this all-embracing concept of service leads to the undervaluing of work and the sorts of problems besetting the likes of Sally. As Christians, we tend to criticize those who 'know the cost of everything and the value of nothing', yet are frequently influenced by the prevailing view in society that unless it costs something, it has no value. This may be the prevailing view of a money-dominated, market-orientated society but it is not the view of scripture. Work has an intrinsic value of its own if it is carried out to satisfy a genuine need. Work for the Christian – paid or unpaid – enables us to glorify and worship God, to participate in his work of creation, sustaining and redemption and to use our God-given talents to his service and the service of others. A view which suggests that a particular person is of greater value because he or she is paid substantially, views work from a totally different, materialist perspective from that of the scriptures.

Strategies for Pastoral Care

Much of what I have written in this chapter has dealt with issues faced by married women – working in the home, returning to paid employment after childbirth, etc. There are certain situations which create difficulties for men as well as women and they are in the sphere of voluntary activity. In my summary below of strategies to adopt, I have focused mainly on people like Sally in churches throughout the country. I hope, however, that you will be able to use some of these strategies, particularly the latter three, when dealing with people like Frank, whose experience of unpaid work is making him feel as undervalued as Sally.

Self-Awareness

The first strategy is directed to you, the carer, and concerns your attitude to women and work. I have summarized above what I believe is the biblical teaching about women in the home, the Church and at work. I have substantiated this with passages from scripture and used the conclusions of others to support my view. Yet I realize that the position is not crystal clear and that opposite views are held by Bible-loving scholars who use the same biblical passages to support diametrically-opposed conclusions. I acknowledge, therefore, that my views may or may not coincide with yours. The crucial thing for all of us to recognize is that our views, especially if they are extreme, can prevent us from providing the sort of pastoral care necessary. If, for example, you share Doug's view that a woman's place is in the home, you must beware of the consequences of offering help to a young mother considering career choice. One of the conditions laid down by Carl Rogers as being essential to effective counselling or therapy is that of unconditional positive regard.[28] It means having a real concern for the person, irrespective of their opinions and attitudes. It has some resemblance to Christian Agape love.

The first strategy, then, in dealing with the controversial issue of 'A woman's place' is to be aware of your own attitudes. Put into practice the motto of the United Reformed Church, *semper reformanda*, always reforming. If you cannot disengage yourself from your attitudes, then refer the person to someone else who can.

Be Sensitive to their Personal Circumstances

Those who come to you for pastoral care are likely to be facing difficulties on a number of fronts. They may be suffering from stress; they may be confused with choice; they may have doubts about their faith; they may be labouring under financial difficulties. In this, as in several of the other areas we have already explored, you must get as much information about their personal circumstances as possible. Is Sally, for example, feeling bad because she is fed up with the mindless tasks being handed to her by Peter and James? Is she feeling angry that Doug has 'volunteered' her for work without consulting her? Is she feeling thwarted because she cannot do what she sees as utterly reasonable? Is she filled with money worries? Is she experiencing guilt because she has such worries? Encourage her to tell you her story before you question, reflect and summarize – but do it sensitively. Be particularly sensitive to the wife of the non-Christian husband or vice versa. You can inflict great harm on their marriage by insisting that one partner attends evening meetings and participates in weekend church activities. Your pastoral role is to support the person, whose spouse is sanctified by their union (1 Corinthians 7:14). Be careful not to undermine the relationship.

Recognize the Need for Affirmation

While we all need to be affirmed, some of us need it more than others! Affirmation costs little and rewards handsomely. As a provider of pastoral care, you can do that by learning what people like Sally are doing, and helping them to see God in it. There is a particularly helpful technique, much used by counsellors, when confronting people who feel undervalued: get them to tell you about someone they have helped, then move them to a seat facing the one they have vacated and say 'thank you for that help'. Do it with them for three or four people that they have helped. In Sally's case, it may refer to some of the young people who have emptied her fridge, will certainly include Peter and James and could possibly be those she has driven in her car from one place to another. Go through the process several times; the impact can be extraordinary. It may be outside your perceived 'terms of reference' as a pastoral carer, but if you are not so restricted, check with Doug how often he affirms Sally and encourage him to increase the frequency of it! Their marriage, like Christine and James', might benefit from help such as attendance at a marriage enrichment programme.

Emphasize the Importance of Using Skills

Voluntary work can often backfire because the person engaged in it is totally demotivated by it. This might be because they cannot see the value of the work itself. It is more likely that they have been allocated work which makes no use of their God-given talents. I well remember a piece of advice given to me by a wise Christian, when my employer had offered me the opportunity to work for a charity for a year. 'Make sure you use your skills,' he counselled, 'for in that way both the charity and you will benefit.' Consider that wise advice when counselling others, for it will prevent frustration and achieve far greater results.

Clarify the Meaning of Service

Christian service is based on the example of Christ, who took on 'the very nature of a servant' (Philippians 2:7) – literally, a slave – in his incarnation. This example of service is to be adopted by his followers, whose greatness 'will be determined by the desire to serve'

(Matthew 20:26–8). This service is to be directed to the entire community using the gifts God gives us to the benefit of others and ultimately to his greater glory (1 Peter 4:10–11). Because it is Christian, service is sacrificial but never degrading. Christ's service

> *did not make him subordinate to other people, but was a free offering of himself, with an acceptance of service and love in return.*[29]

Service is not a Christian activity predominantly carried out by women or male ministers of the Church. It is to be the hallmark of all who follow Jesus, both as individuals and as a community. And note, last of all, that such service does not result in bondage but creates, in the words of the *Book of Common Prayer*, 'perfect freedom'.

10

PROVIDING CARE

Carry each other's burdens, and in this way you will fulfil the law of Christ.
(Galatians 6:2)

And now let us turn to the final character at our meeting: Peter, the minister, who had called the other six people together in the first place.

Peter's Story

Peter, like Tom, is 50. He and his wife, Anne, have three grown-up children – twins and a younger son. One of the twins suffered from brain damage at birth, attended special schools throughout his childhood and adolescence and now lives in a residential home run by a Christian charity. His twin sister has recently qualified as a teacher but so far has only managed to obtain a temporary post. The younger son is at university reading media studies, a subject which his father finds perplexing and slightly embarrassing.

Peter was ordained in his late 20s after three years at theological college. Anne and he had married before he started college and she had given birth to the twins during their time there. The support they had received from colleagues and staff had enabled them to cope with the trauma of a severely handicapped child. They count several of those erstwhile students as their closest friends, even though they see them infrequently.

Ever since ordination, Peter has been engaged in parochial ministry which – by and large – has given him great satisfaction. He has never seriously contemplated any other form of ministry, not least because he finds change unsettling and disturbing. Yet he has not been able to hide from change – there have been many changes in the Church since his ordination. Some of these have caused him great concern. The rise of the home groups, now commonplace but then a radical departure, seemed to Peter to threaten his own authority. The charismatic movement had, in many instances, created division rather than unity and, while he believed the movement to be from God, he deplored some of the bitterness it had engendered. The ordination of women had precipitated in him a personal crisis which he had shared with no one. He felt his biblical theology and his sexual identity being undermined. To add to all this, there is now a debate in progress about changes in the clergy freehold which may threaten his security and, more importantly, his freedom to exercise his ministry.

Next to God, Anne has been his source of comfort and support for many, many years. She nurtured their handicapped son magnificently and is very close to the other two. This is a great relief to Peter for their daughter is worried about her future prospects and the younger son has adopted a lifestyle which Peter chooses to ignore. Yet even Anne – dependable, rock-like Anne – has caught the disease of change. She had, for example, read the papers he had been sent in advance of the deanery training day on feminist theology and was clearly fascinated by the contents. Peter had given cursory attention to those same documents and had sat through the session uncomfortably conscious that the old divisions within the Church – conservative, liberal, high and low – no longer seemed to count on this subject. Anne had quizzed him on his return but had said little on the subject since. He had noticed, however, that she was ordering books from the library by authors he had never heard of, and whose contents he had no desire to study. He had also noticed the leaflet in the diary for a day course on Beguine Spirituality, whatever that might be.

For most of the time, Peter believes he is in the place that God wants him to be but he is experiencing more and more doubts and is not at peace. Like Tom, he has lost some of the motivation he once had. Like Nick, he is questioning his vocation. Like Monica, he is under a great deal of stress.

The Pastor's Role

I could go on suggesting the range of work-related issues he is having to confront. Clergy, pastors, ministers – call them what you will – are as likely to run the same gamut of experiences as those of us whose workplace is outside the Church. In many instances, they have to cope with much more, a point well documented in Mary Anne Coate's book on the subject.[1]

There is, however, a major difference between the role discharged by Peter in his daily work and that discharged by Nick or Sally or Monica. It is that the former believes he has a responsibility for pastoral care towards the latter and, as far as he is aware, the latter share that belief with him. This is a crucial issue as far as the provision of pastoral care is concerned.

In this chapter, therefore, I intend to use Peter's situation as the means of answering the question posed at the very beginning of the book, namely, how is pastoral care provided to church members who are encountering difficulties in or with their work? What, in other words, should Peter do in order to meet the needs of his six colleagues?

What is Pastoral Care?

It may seem strange at this stage of the book to spend time on the subject of pastoral care when I have used these two words time and time again without any form of explanation. The reason is that I want to make explicit what has been implicit in all the earlier chapters and, by so doing, to focus our attention on the following highly practical questions:

Who might be the recipients of pastoral care in the context of the work-related issues we have discussed?

What form does such pastoral care take?

Who are the providers and how are they best equipped for this ministry?

Here, then, are two definitions of pastoral care drawn from the same two reference books used when we set out to discover the biblical meaning of work. The first definition is by Roger Hurding, who suggests that pastoral care is

> the practical outworking of the Church's concern for the everyday and the ultimate needs of its members and the wider community.[2]

Alastair Campbell, the other author, defines it as

> That aspect of the ministry of the Church which is concerned with the well-being of individuals and of communities.[3]

The definitions are similar and highlight three distinct points:

Pastoral Care is Exercised by the Church

It is a ministry exercised by the whole Church and not by one individual person. It is not the sole preserve of the pastor (despite the name) or the curate (whose title may also suggest it). Quite the reverse, asserts Frank Lake, as he argues against the unbiblical notion of 'separate clergymen working like therapists or general practitioners in isolation from the therapeutic community of the Body of Christ'. Pastoral care is the preserve of the whole Church.

> *The resources of God are mediated in the whole life of the Christian fellowship, gathered to hear and study the Word of God, gathered round the Lord's table where his Body sustains them, gathered in fellowship for mutual help and counsel.*[4]

Pastoral care will be provided by specific members of the church but they act on behalf of the whole Church and not as representatives of the church leadership. It is a corporate rather than an individual ministry.

Because it is exercised by the Church it is specifically Christian. The words 'pastoral care' are not used exclusively in a church or Christian setting. An article in the *Handbook of Counselling in Britain*,[5] for example, uses the words frequently but not about an overtly Christian ministry. Pastoral care may refer to education, for those in the educational sphere often use the phrase to describe the welfare aspect of schooling which may be – but often is not – provided by a Christian.

Throughout this book, the definition of pastoral care is decidedly Christian because, to borrow some adjectives from Michael Taylor[6] it is supportive, informative and transformative. It is supported by the faith of the Christian provider; it is informed by the scriptures and it leads to the transformation of the person in his or her journey towards the fullness of Christ.

Pastoral Care is Directed Towards Individuals and Community

An earlier book in this series, *Counselling in Context*, highlighted the tendency to equate pastoral care with pastoral counselling.[7] This severely limits the domain of pastoral care and suggests that all involved in it should be trained therapists. There are, of course, many aspects of pastoral care which involve one-to-one encounters with another person. All the so-called presenting problems I have introduced in this book have derived from a person's discomfort arising from his or her daily activities. Yet, as we have already noted, some of this discomfort is exacerbated, if not originally caused, by external influences.

One such influence is the inadequate teaching on several of the matters we have considered and which is usually given to groups or to the whole Christian community. Furthermore, there are certain aspects of pastoral care which are concerned with the structures of the society in which we live or the organizations in which we work. Pastoral care in such cases may mean our acting in solidarity with others to right a wrong. It may involve our discharging a prophetic role by publicly denouncing injustice and oppression. These aspects, while they may originate in the desire to support one particular person, bring us into close contact with a much wider cross-section of people and not with church members only. This raises the important question of whether we offer pastoral care to the wider community. We will return to that question soon but first we need to look at the third feature of pastoral care included in the definition.

Pastoral Care is Concerned with the Needs of the Whole Person

In the article from which I have already quoted, Roger Hurding uses four biblical metaphors to describe the varieties of Christian pastoral care.[8] The prophet challenges, instructs and calls to repentance; the shepherd comforts and supports, the priest identifies with others and provides forgiveness; the physician heals. 'Go to the poor,' urges Richard Baxter, 'see what they want, and show your compassion at once to their soul and body.'[9] Such pastoral care provides for the whole person – body, soul, mind and spirit – and not just for one particular aspect of it. It is directed at people in their relationship to God, to each other and to the world in which they live.

Who are the Recipients of Pastoral Care?

When we are commanded to take heed to all the flock, it is plainly implied that flocks must ordinarily be no greater than we are capable of overseeing, or taking heed to.[10]

When Richard Baxter wrote these words he was ministering in Kidderminster, a town of 800 houses and 2000 people. He regarded all the inhabitants of that town as his flock and, as we know, God blessed his ministry in a marvellous way. For us, living in a very different world 350 years later, Baxter's words raise two crucial matters.

The first is whether pastoral care should only be offered to those who are members of the church. The answer may well be taken on logistical grounds. There is, as Baxter points out, a limit on our capability to provide care; one way of imposing that limit is to restrict pastoral care to church members. But what does that say to those outside the church? Here we are faced with a theological rather than a logistical challenge. If we limit our care to the 'insider', what of those on the periphery or who are outside? Monica will obviously be included but what of her husband, Alf? Nick is plainly eligible but his father, presumably, is not. And what of those who have little, if any, contact with the church, other than through the occasional offices or when in severe distress? Do we exclude them from pastoral care?

The answer we give to these questions will depend to a large extent on how we view the nature of ministry – of how we see God at work in the world. If we take a convergent, church-centred view, we will restrict pastoral care to members. Our energies and our time will be devoted to the well-being of those of the household of faith. This approach is entirely consistent with the separatist, 'Christ against culture' response to work which I introduced in chapter three. It has a good pedigree, not least among evangelicals.

If, however, our view is divergent or world-centred we will want to extend care to others. We will seek to help *all* who are suffering loss through redundancy, not only Frank; we will get alongside *anyone* who is bowed down with the burden of stress, not only Monica.

Each of the churches you attend has to debate this matter and resolve it for itself. I urge you to consider the message you are sending both to church members and those outside when you arrive at your decision.

What Form does Pastoral Care Take?

Pastoral care, according to the two definitions above and our discussion so far, can embrace activities as diverse as political lobbying and spiritual direction; the former tackles the ills of society, the latter focuses on the well-being of the person. As far as work-related issues are concerned, I am going to restrict my comments to three areas of activity in which Christians are commonly involved. By this I am not joining the ranks of the 'separatists'. Rather, I want to point out the vehicles which already exist and from which we can offer pastoral care either to those within or outside the church.

Public Worship

Public communal worship provides the opportunity for the people of God to praise God the Father, God the Son and God the Holy Spirit. It is the occasion when the Bride of Christ claims her love for her husband, when the body of Christ submits itself to its divine head (Ephesians 5:23). Worship must always be directed towards God and any activity or person which detracts from that dishonours the Godhead.

In order to worship God correctly we have to learn about him, and there is a profound sense in which worship instructs our faith. The faith of countless people has been formed by the Psalms, the *Book of Common Prayer*, the hymns of Charles Wesley and the sermons of influential preachers. This has all happened in the context of worship and influences our beliefs, our attitudes and our lifestyle. It affects the way we experience God and relate to him. It moulds our image of the divine. It has a major impact on our approach towards the world in which we live and the people we encounter. It shapes our understanding of, and our response to, work.

The conduct and the content of worship will have one of three effects on the worshipper's view of work as well as the pastoral care we might offer. It may support the biblical view we encountered in chapter two, or it may distort that view. Alternatively, it may adopt a Laodicean neutrality by ignoring it altogether. The evidence we noted at the very beginning of this book suggests that the third position is the one most commonly adopted.

If our pastoral care for those facing up to difficulties at, or with, work is to be effective then work must be more central in our worship – in our preaching, in our teaching, in our singing, in our choice of readings and in our celebration of the Holy Communion.

Teaching

The importance of biblical teaching has been stated repeatedly in this book. Its significance in pastoral care was highlighted by Richard Baxter in *The Reformed Pastor*, that 'incomparable treatise'[11] from which I have already quoted. Throughout that work, he urged the pastor to teach through sermons, smaller meetings and catechizing. Baxter lived in a world very different from our own. The whole approach to teaching and instruction has changed since his time. Now we talk more about learning, putting the emphasis on the receiver rather than the giver. This shift in emphasis is addressed by Alastair Campbell in his book *Rediscovering Pastoral Care*.[12] He suggests we move from 'indoctrination', with its underlying assumption of unquestioning acceptance, to 'exploration', which evokes a questioning and searching response in the learner. But he does not stop there. He introduces a third word, 'companionship', which recognizes that 'teacher' and 'pupil' are 'fellow travellers, friends and comrades on their journey.'[13] Interestingly, Campbell's three words approximate to Baxter's three teaching modes and fit with our division between worship, fellowship and relationship.

It is impracticable to incorporate this 'companionship' or even the 'exploration' into our worship. It was the same for Baxter and the practice of catechizing he so strongly encouraged. Their rightful place is in the group or the one-to-one encounter. The key is to ensure that all three modes of teaching are congruent, supporting each other in such a way that what is spoken from the pulpit is tested through questioning and achieved in our daily activity.

Holy Communion

As a young Christian raised in a conservative evangelical church, I struggled with the meaning of what happened at the consecration and thereafter. I learned the distinction between remembrance and memorial and developed the doctrinal antennae necessary to detect the slightest hint of transubstantiation or consubstantiation. My views and my experience were influenced by the 1662 *Book of Common Prayer* and the doctrinal emphasis of Cranmer, whose version of a century before had only been slightly revised. Time has passed, and the Holy Communion service has changed. An earlier form of eucharistic worship has been adopted by the Protestant and Roman Catholic Church. The corporate nature of the latter has replaced the more personal nature of the former. Holy Communion has become the central act of worship in many evangelical churches.

Two communion prayers are of particular relevance to our topic of pastoral care and work. The first is an ancient prayer of consecration included in the liturgy of the Church of South India and used in many Anglican churches.

Blessed are you Lord, God of all creation.
Through your goodness we have this bread and wine to offer,
fruit of the earth and the work of human hands.
They will become for us the Bread of Life and the Cup of Salvation.

The second is the thanksgiving and dedicatory prayer after the communion itself:

Almighty God,
we thank you for feeding us
with the body and blood of your Son Jesus Christ.
Through him we offer you our souls and bodies
to be a living sacrifice.
Send us out in the power of your Spirit
to live and work
to your praise and glory.
Amen.[14]

In these two prayers we see the intermingling of divine and human work in creation, in sustaining and in redemption. The quality of our pastoral care and the understanding of those to whom we offer it will be fashioned by these prayers.

Group Fellowship

The second locus for pastoral care is the group – the church-based home group or the work-based Christian group. Whereas public worship forms the attitudes and beliefs of the whole Church, the smaller group can challenge and debate these in a way which is impossible when the whole congregation is present. This is Alastair Campbell's 'exploration' I referred to earlier. There is, by definition, much greater intimacy and focus within these groups simply because of their size. Greater intimacy allows a person to share with others that which is of concern; greater focus enables the group to give their whole attention to the topic being raised.

The value of the church-based home group is that it is made up of those who are members of the same church, and so can forge effective links between services on a Sunday and service during the week. The people present are likely to know one another and each other's family situation because of this regular contact. The value of the work-based Christian group, on the other hand, is that the people present understand the issues at stake much better than those of the home group, quite simply because they are more closely involved in it. These groups may be employer based (such as a company's Christian Fellowship), associated with a particular professional body (lawyers and doctors, for example), or even located in a particular work district such as exist in some large cities.

Groups can be used for pastoral care in two ways; the first is to aid understanding, the second to provide support. To fulfil the function of aiding understanding, instructional materials are required. Examples of these are contained in Graham Dow's booklet, from which I quoted earlier.[15] More can be found at the end of each chapter of Thomas Smith's *God On The Job*.[16] Alternatively, you could create your own resources to ensure that they are rooted appropriately in the soil of local experience.

To fulfil the function of providing support, sensitive leadership is needed. Whereas some may be helped by sharing their work-related problems with others, not everyone will. We can learn again from Baxter. The person providing pastoral care should be familiar with the Word of God, given to meditation and prayer and should

> *know every person that belongeth to our charge … for if we know not their temperament or disease, we are not likely to prove successful physicians.*[17]

One-to-One Relationships

The following three models of individual pastoral care all fit into Campbell's 'companionship' model. They might be conducted by the same person or they might not. They are alternatives which can be selected to meet specific sets of circumstances. The best way to view them is along a continuum showing that they are neither more important nor less important than each other.

The Neighbour

The neighbour is the one described by Jesus in St Luke's gospel as the person who recognizes another's need and takes practical action to meet that need (Luke 10:29–37). This may be the most common example of pastoral care, for it can happen at any place and at any time. It may be structured in the sense that a meeting is arranged beforehand, or it may be casual with a meeting brought about as the result of a chance (or providential) encounter.

The Counsellor

The growth in counselling in recent years has been exponential. The difference between this and the neighbour model is the difference between formality and informality. Counselling is characterized by the following:

It is planned in advance.

Meetings take place at regular intervals.

It is restricted by time boundaries.

A contract of confidentiality is maintained.

Fees may be paid.

The Spiritual Director

The spiritual director is more commonly associated with the Orthodox or the Roman Catholic Church and far less frequently with the Protestant Church, especially evangelicals. This is changing and many are finding that the rule of St Benedict which influenced Cranmer so much in the compilation of the *Book of Common Prayer*, or the Spiritual Exercises of St Ignatius which encourage extensive meditation on the word of God, are neither as suspect or misleading as we used to think them.[18]

There are a number of similarities between spiritual direction and counselling. The director uses many of the same skills as the counsellor such as listening, reflecting and creating empathy. Meetings, planned in advance, tend to be of the same duration although less frequent. Confidentiality is vital.

The two practices, however, differ in a number of important respects. In the first place, counselling focuses on the person and his or her problem whereas spiritual direction is God centred. The objective of the former is to deal with a particular difficult issue, the objective of the latter is to walk more closely with God. Secondly, the aim of counselling is wholeness in terms of mental or psychological well-being, whereas the aim of spiritual direction is holiness in terms of relationship with God. So, for example, the person suffering from depression will go to the counsellor to help them tackle their depression, whereas the same person will go to the spiritual director to discover what God is saying to them through their depression. Thirdly, the counsellor draws heavily on the insights of psychology and psychoanalysis to support his or her work, whereas the spiritual director relies more on the scriptures and on Christian tradition. One is not better than the other; they are different.

Who are the Providers of Pastoral Care?

The last of our questions is a crucial one for any church as it plans its programme of pastoral care. We have already noted that care is the ministry of the whole Church and not that of a few people. I suggested earlier that we looked at pastoral care in terms of worship, group fellowship and one-to-one relationships. Responsibility for worship is, in most churches, well defined. House groups have been in existence for many years and experienced leaders abound.

When we turn to the question of one-to-one relationships, however, the picture is less clear. Responsibility for this is not the sole preserve of the Church leadership or the ordained clergy, although many among this group properly see it as a major part of their ministry. Yet, it cannot be their sole preserve for three reasons.

The first is that they will be unable to devote sufficient time to it. The second is that the locus of their work is usually the local church. Because of this they are often 'inadvertently equipping us to support their ministry rather than equipping us to do the work of ours'.[19] The third is that they do not always see the link between divine and human work — a shortcoming illustrated in the story of Graham Dow's theological students.

Nor is it the exclusive domain of the professional. Certainly, there are some basic skills and special knowledge which will enhance those which the carer offers, but skills can be learned and knowledge can be acquired. There are, though, a number of personal characteristics which are important for those who engage in this ministry on a one-to-one basis.

A genuine desire to work with one other person is necessary. This is not a universal gift nor is it an essential feature of being a Christian. Some Christians relate best with small or substantial groups, others are more comfortable on a one-to-one basis. We are all different and our gifts are capable of being used in different ways. For this task the preference for one-to-one encounters is an important characteristic.

A second characteristic required is the ability to keep confidences. If this is difficult for you, avoid situations where it is expected of you. The capacity to maintain personal detachment is also important. The preacher in Ecclesiastes reminds us that there is a time to cry and a time to laugh (Ecclesiastes 3:4). Today we might call that empathy — the ability to stand in another person's shoes, to get into (not under) their skin. There are, however, dangers in such identification if it results in your inability to disengage with the situation. The carer who takes upon himself or herself the burdens of the other person soon loses their own effectiveness in their role.

Another characteristic needed is the willingness to devote time to another person. Pastoral care can consume a substantial amount of a person's time and energy. If you are motivated by achievement, the task of getting alongside and travelling with another towards an uncertain destination can be tiresome and frustrating.

Strategies for Pastoral Care

I will conclude this chapter with a summary of the key points to consider in developing a programme of pastoral care which addresses work-related issues. Most of these points have been introduced in earlier chapters. I put them forward here as features which should characterize our pastoral care. They are offered for your review and debate.

The Local Church at Worship

Our pastoral care directed towards those at work will be most effective when our praise and our preaching:

honours God as a worker

recognizes people as his co-workers

nourishes the whole person active in God's world

fits each person for service in his or her place of work.

The Smaller Group in Fellowship

Our pastoral care offered to those at work will be enhanced by:

encouraging home groups to study the subject of work

training home group leaders to handle work-related issues sensitively

compiling a list of work-based Christian groups for reference purposes.

People in One-to-One Relationships

Our pastoral care to support those with work-related problems can be put into effect by:

providing training in the basic skills common to counselling and spiritual direction

choosing appropriate people from within the local church as counsellors or spiritual directors

ensuring that they have the necessary training

subsidising their supervision

identifying alternative resources outside the local church.

Finally, the availability of pastoral care must be made known to the entire church membership and, if you choose to develop the ministry in this way, to the wider community outside.

Our study of the subject of pastoral care and work started with the story of a church meeting. It will end by revisiting that meeting at the point we left it.

Part Four

WORK EXPECTATIONS

11

THE FUTURE OF WORK

Seven heads bowed.

> 'Loving Father, be with us as we come together. Help us to
> lay aside the trials and tribulations of everyday life. Give
> us wisdom and strength as we plan to further your work in
> this place. Amen.'

Seven heads were raised. Seven pairs of hands shuffled seven
sets of agenda papers. The meeting had begun.

'Thank you so much for coming along at such short
notice,' said Peter. 'You are probably wondering why it is
that I have invited the six of you. The fact is I want to discuss
the subject of the future of work.'

'Wait a minute,' said Tom, brandishing his agenda
papers, 'the note you sent round was about pastoral care.
What on earth has work got to do with that?'

'A great deal,' replied Peter, 'although we don't often
make the connection. Take your own situation, for example,
Tom. You have come straight from work. I guess you have
been there for 12 hours. You look distressed.'

'Distressed?' shouted Tom, 'of course I'm distressed. If
you only knew what I'm having to cope with at the moment,
you'd be distressed.'

'Precisely,' responded Peter. He was quaking as he

looked at Tom but he knew that, for once, he had to be assertive or nothing would be achieved. 'I don't know what you are having to cope with at the moment for the simple reason that you have not told me. If I were a gambling man, I'd bet against you having told anyone about your work.'

'You don't need to bet, you're quite right,' responded Tom, surprised that Peter had not retreated at his initial outburst. 'But I still don't get the connection between pastoral care and the future of work.'

'Neither do I,' added Frank, 'especially for those of us whose work is something that happened in the past. The future is all about *not* working.'

'OK,' said Peter, 'let me explain. A couple of weeks ago I attended the quarterly meeting of the ministers from all the churches in this town. Geoffrey, the pastor of the Baptist church, had just come back from a sabbatical and spoke to us on the subject he had been studying.'

'Sabbatical,' sneered Tom, 'you clergy don't know what work is about. Do you know that in the last four years—'

'Oh please, Tom,' interrupted Sally, 'please let Peter continue.'

Tom stopped. What was going on here? First Peter confronts him and then Sally interrupts him – Sally who usually wouldn't say boo to a goose. This was not going to be an easy meeting. He stopped talking and stared grimly at Peter, challenging him to continue.

'Geoffrey has been studying the changes in our social structures as the basis of developing appropriate evangelistic outreach. A lot of what he said was interesting but made little impression on me. When he started to talk about the changes in patterns of work, however, he really held my attention and I came away determined to do something about it.'

'I don't follow you,' said Christine. 'What can you do about the changing patterns of work?'

Peter ignored the criticism implied by the tone of the question and went on.

'Let's take some examples. Frank, when you started work with the bank, what were your expectations?'

Frank paused for a moment, turning back the pages of his memory to his teenage years. Then he spoke.

'Security, I suppose, was the most important thing. I was born during the Second World War. My parents had experienced the uncertainties of the '30s and the instability of the war. The job at the bank offered a sense of stability for the present and certainty for the future.'

'And did the bank live up to those expectations?'

'For the first 30 years it did; then it all changed. It betrayed me.'

'Betrayed – that's a strong word. You had given 30 or more years of your life to that organization and then suddenly you were no longer wanted. The stability and the security you expected in the first place, and which had been around for many years, simply disappeared.'

'I would rather not talk about it in public,' murmured Frank.

'I understand – I'm sorry that it still hurts. Let me move on then. Nick, you have been with your employer for about 18 months. Do you expect to stay with them for all your working life?'

'Of course not,' replied Nick, 'I'll stay for as long as I enjoy the work and gain useful experience. The average period that people like me stay with the company is three to four years.'

'And then?' asked Peter.

'Oh, I'll move on to something else using the skills I have gained to take on more responsibility. That's normal for people of my age. We are concerned with keeping ourselves employable and the only way we can do that is to keep our knowledge and our skills up to date and in demand.'

'That's an interesting point,' said Christine. 'If I recall

correctly, it is a similar one made a few years ago in the Social Justice Commission report. I thought it was revolutionary thinking but it seems to have become conventional wisdom.'

'What report and what revolution?' questioned Frank. 'I'm lost.'

'The Social Justice report,' explained Christine, 'was prepared by a body set up by John Smith when he became the leader of the Labour Party in the UK. Sadly, he died before it was published. The report identified three great revolutions which are transforming our world. One of these – I can't remember the order in which they came – is the economic revolution. Such has been the worldwide change in recent years that finance, technology and skills are now international – or 'global' as the report had it. One consequence of this change is that no one can expect a job for life any more. This is because change is continuous and jobs, like money and technology, can be moved from country to country. All in all, that means we have to become like Nick and keep on updating our skills. If not, we join the dinosaurs.'

'Exactly,' responded Nick. 'It's nice to learn that your party actually got something right for once.'

Christine grimaced but it was Tom who spoke.

'But what about loyalty?' he demanded. 'Surely you owe something to the company?'

'Yes, I do, but loyalty has to be mutual. The company I am with cannot guarantee the sort of long-term future that Frank spoke about. I'm loyal to it while I'm there but I don't feel that I have to repay some sort of debt.'

'Thank you, Nick,' interrupted Peter. 'Your expectations compared with Frank's illustrate one of the points made by Geoffrey. In our present world and in the future, jobs will not be for life and careers will involve moving from one organization to another. The consequences of this, as Christine has reminded us, are that we have to keep on developing new skills so that we can remain employable. Which brings me to the next point.'

'Wait a minute, Vicar,' interrupted Monica. Everyone stared. Monica never interrupted. Indeed, she hardly ever spoke. She was visibly trembling, whether with anger or fear Peter did not know, but he realized the significance of the moment and motioned her to speak.

'I have listened to what you and the others have said. I'm sure it all makes sense as far as someone like Nick is concerned. He's all right. He's had a good education and has a well-paid job, but what about the thousands who aren't like him? What about my Alf who's been out of work for five years and my Darren who has never been in it? What does the future hold for them?'

There was silence. Monica was close to tears; everyone was conscious of it and somewhat embarrassed by it. Peter knew that he had to handle the next few moments with extreme sensitivity and was formulating an appropriate sentence when Sally spoke. She looked straight at Monica.

'I want to thank you, Monica, for what you have said. I could never have said it. You are very brave.' Then, turning to the others, she continued 'I think that Monica's question demonstrates beyond doubt the importance of the topic that Peter has raised. I haven't read the report that Christine referred to but it's as clear as daylight that the society in which we live has changed out of all recognition in only a few years. It seems to me that we are fast becoming a society of haves and have-nots. The haves are represented by Nick — and this is not personal criticism, Nick — who can look forward to a prosperous future using their skills, expanding their experience and receiving ever fatter wage packets. The have-nots are the likes of Darren who have no work and see no hope of getting any. Their future — and there are more of them than the others — is one of hopelessness.'

'I can't accept that,' said Tom. 'If business men like me were encouraged by the government to invest in the long-term future there would be jobs for all those who wanted them. Full employment would be achievable once more.'

'I doubt it, Tom,' remarked Peter. 'At our meeting, Geoffrey presented some interesting figures as to what has happened in employment in the post-war period. The full employment scene familiar to people like you and me was full male employment. Men worked 40 hours or more a week in the factories or the offices, earning enough money for their wife, who looked after the home and the children. Millions of those jobs have disappeared. The jobs that have replaced them are mainly part-time and are carried out predominantly by women. There is no likelihood at all of returning to those days of full employment in the way we experienced it.'

'That's not much comfort to me,' murmured Monica, 'I thought we were meant to be discussing caring for others not rubbing salt in their wounds.'

'You're right,' said Christine, 'we are discussing pastoral care. But Peter is right too, for we have to face up to reality. If we pretend that all will be well tomorrow, we make the situation worse rather than better. Somehow or other, we Christians have got to face up to these problems at two levels. We have to address the structures, which is my short-hand for saying that we should be working towards a just society, and we have to follow Christ and take our place with those who are suffering, sharing what we have with those who are deprived.'

'You're on one of your hobbyhorses again, Christine,' smiled Sally, 'and I'm sure you're right. But as I see it, our task is not to sort out the world's problems but to provide support for Monica and for you and for me.' She turned to Peter.

'Did your friend Geoffrey come up with any answers?'

'No, sadly,' responded Peter, 'but he did identify more changes. New technology, for example, has already changed so much of what we do and how we work. In some places, people already order their shopping by looking at the television screen and then pay for it without moving from the living room. More and more people are working at home, linked by telephone to their employer's computer network. Using videos and other gadgetry for education is no longer a fringe activity. It's reality.'

'All of which sounds like hell on earth to me,' muttered Frank. 'The thing I miss most about work is the companionship of colleagues. The picture you're painting looks as though my successors in the bank will be working from home. That's a terrible thought.'

'Perhaps,' said Peter, 'but perhaps not. Home-working – or tele-working – is increasing every day and with it comes great social change. As Christians, one of our challenges is to help create the sort of community which will provide companionship for those who work on their own.'

'And what about those like my Alf who have no work and cannot meet with others because he has no money and no dignity left? What about him and my Darren? What is the Church going to do for them?'

'I wish I had the answer, but I'm afraid I don't. I want to search for the solutions – several solutions, I guess – but I need your help and your support. The challenge, as I see it, is to provide pastoral care to the whole church or even to the whole community. We do that well in some instances but we do it atrociously in others. Your work among the Guides, Monica, is an example of what we do really well and so is yours, Sally, with the young mothers who have recently moved into the area. But we do very little for Tom at his engineering company or Nick in the city or for you, Monica, in the chemicals factory. And we don't even contemplate the difficulties of Alf and Darren. We are not alone in this, but now we have a great opportunity. We are experiencing a new revolution in the way we earn our living, which for many of us will be painful. Our challenge is to discover, and then put into practice, the best ways we can help those of our members, and those outside, to find God in our daily activities.'

There was a pause. The silence was broken by Tom.

'I'll buy that, Peter. It's an enormous challenge but we've got to face up to it.' And then he added, 'For God's sake.'

'I'd like to take part too,' said Monica. 'I'm not sure what I have to offer but I need help and so do lots more people I know.'

Frank, Christine, Sally and Nick nodded their assent. Then Nick asked the question they were all asking themselves.

'What do we do next?'

'I'm glad you asked,' said Peter, 'for I would like all of you to think about the points contained in the handout Geoffrey gave to the ministers' meeting.'

He passed the paper round.

'In it you will find some of the issues we have already raised, and many more besides.'

'And when we have worked through it?' asked Frank.

Peter smiled.

'It will be time for another meeting – but this time we will work from the same agenda.'

REFERENCES

1 Meeting the Problems

1 Yearsley, Ian, 'Industrial Mission: a Resource for Readers', *The Reader*, vol. XCII, no. 1 (Spring 1995), p. 7.
2 Greene, Mark, *Thank God it's Monday*, Scripture Union, 1994.
3 Dow, Graham, *A Christian Understanding of Daily Work*, Grove Books, 1994, p. 3.
4 *ibid.*, p. 20.

2 The Biblical View of Work

1 Marshall, P. A., 'Work', *New Dictionary of Christian Ethics and Pastoral Theology*, ed. Atkinson, David J. and Field, David H., IVP, 1995, pp. 898–900.
2 Atherton, John R., 'Work', *A Dictionary of Pastoral Care*, ed. Campbell, Alistair V., SPCK, 1987, pp. 296–7.
3 Goldingay, John, 'God at Work in Genesis 1', *God at Work*, Goldingay, John and Innes, Robert, Grove Books, 1994, pp. 3–5.
4 von Rad, Gerhard, *Genesis*, SCM Press, 1972, p. 61.
5 Stott, John R. W., *The Message of Romans*, IVP, 1994, p. 73.
6 Sayers, Dorothy L., *The Mind of the Maker*, Mowbray, 1994, p. 38.
7 Collect for 8th Sunday after Trinity, *The Book of Common Prayer*.

8 Motyer, J. A., *The Prophecy of Isaiah*, IVP, 1993, p. 321.

9 *ibid.*, p. 314.

10 Fowler, James W., *Faith Development and Pastoral Care*, Fortress Press, 1987, p. 38.

11 *ibid.*

12 quoted in Goldingay, John, *art. cit.*, p. 11.

13 Moltmann, Jurgen, *God in Creation*, SCM Press, 1985, p. 279.

14 Hoekema, Anthony A., *Created in God's Image*, Wm B. Eerdmans, 1986, p. 67.

15 *ibid.*, p. 68.

16 Moltmann, Jurgen, *op. cit.*, pp. 219, 220.

17 Eichrodt, Walther, *Theology of the Old Testament*, vol. ii, SCM Press, 1967, p. 127.

18 *ibid.*

19 Pope John Paul II, *Laborem Exercens*, Catholic Truth Society, 1981, p. 33.

20 Dow, Graham, *A Christian Understanding of Daily Work*, Grove Books, 1994, p. 20.

21 Stott, John R. W., *Issues facing Christians Today*, Marshall Pickering, 1990, p. 167.

22 Richardson, Alan, 'Work', *A Theological Word Book of the Bible*, ed. Richardson, Alan, SCM Press, 1957, pp. 285–7.

23 *See* introduction by Susan Howatch, Somerset Ward, R., *To Jerusalem*, Mowbray, 1994, p. viii.

24 Greene, Mark, *op. cit.*, pp. 96ff.

25 de Waal, Esther, *A World Made Whole*, Fount, 1991, pp. 68ff.

26 Brother Lawrence, *The Practice of the Presence of God*, Mowbray, 1977, p. 23.

27 Calvin, John, *The Gospel According To St John 1–10*, Oliver & Boyd, 1959, p. 124.

28 Berkouwer, G. C., *Man: the image of God*, Wm B. Eerdmans, 1962; Carey, George, *I Believe in Man*, Hodder & Stoughton, 1977; Hoekema, Anthony A., *Created in God's Image*, Wm B. Eerdmans, 1986.

29 *ibid.*, p. 213.

30 *ibid.*, p. 216.

31 Carey, George, *op. cit.*, p. 50.

32 Hodge, Charles, *Romans*, The Banner of Truth Trust, 1972, p. 40.

33 Schumacher, E. F., *Small is Beautiful*, Sphere Books, 1974.

34 Schumacher, E. F., *Good Work*, Sphere Books, 1982, pp. 3, 4.

35 Schumacher, Christian, *To Live and Work*, Marc Europe, 1987.

36 Turner, Francis, 'Co-Workers in His Design', *The Way*, vol. XXIII, no. 3 (July 1983), p. 172.

37 Eaton, Michael A., *Ecclesiastes*, IVP, 1983, p. 46.

38 Hendriksen, William, *An Exposition of the Gospel of St John*, Banner of Truth, 1959, p. 85.

39 Carey, George, *op. cit.*, pp. 62ff.

40 Wright, N. T., *The Epistles of Paul to the Colossians and to Philemon*, IVP, 1986, p. 73.

41 Letham, Robert, *The Work of Christ*, IVP, 1993, p. 202.

42 Westcott, B. F., *The Gospel According to St John*, John Murray, 1902, p. 84.

43 Hoekema, Anthony A., *op. cit.*, p. 65.

44 Arendt, Hannah, *The Human Condition*, The University of Chicago Press, 1958.

45 *ibid.*, p. 80.

3 A Change in Outlook

1 Squire, Aelred, *Asking the Fathers*, SPCK, 1973.

2 Fox, Matthew, *The Reinvention of Work*, HarperCollins, 1994.

3 *ibid.*, p. 1.

4 Marshall, P. A., *op. cit.*, p. 900.

5 McGrath, Alister, *Roots that Refresh*, Hodder & Stoughton, 1991, p. 140.

6 *ibid.*, p. 145.

7 Calvin, John, *A Harmony of the Gospels*, The St Andrew Press, 1972, vol. 2, p. 288.

8 *The Homilies*, Focus Christian Ministries, 1986.

9 *ibid.*, p. 360.

10 Barth, Karl, *Protestant Theology in the Nineteenth Century*, SCM Press, 1972.

11 *ibid.*, p. 37.

12 *ibid.*, p. 38.

13 Cragg, Gerald R., *The Church and the Age of Reason 1648–1789*, Penguin, 1977, p. 75.

14 *ibid.*, p. 76.

15 Newbigin, Lesslie, *Foolishness to the Greeks*, SPCK, 1986, p. 24.

16 Appleyard, Bryan, *Understanding the Present*, Pan Books, 1993, p. 28.

17 Cragg, *op. cit.*, p. 43.

18 Hill, Christopher, *The English Bible and the 17th Century Revolution*, Penguin, 1993, p. 18.

19 Kent, John H. S., 'Christian Theology in the 18th to 20th centuries', *A History of Christian Doctrine*, ed. Cunliffe-Jones, Hubert, with Drewery, Benjamin, T. & T. Clark, 1980, p. 461.

20 Appleyard, Bryan, *op. cit.*, p. 92.

21 Smith, Adam, *The Wealth of Nations*, Penguin, 1986, pp. 109, 110.

22 Pope John Paul II, *op. cit.*, p. 44.

23 For a discussion on this subject, *see* Laurence, Anne, *Women in England*, Weidenfeld & Nicolson, 1944, pp. 108ff.

24 Porter, Roy, *English Society in the 18th Century*, Penguin, 1982, p. 32.

25 Bridges, William, *Jobshift*, Nicholas Brealey Publishing, 1994, p. 34.

26 Niebuhr, Richard H., *Christ and Culture*, Harper & Row, 1951.

27 Wainwright, Geoffrey, *Doxology*, Epworth Press, 1982, pp. 384ff.

28 Wainwright, Geoffrey, 'Types of Spirituality', *The Study of Spirituality*, ed. Jones, Cheslyn, Wainwright, Geoffrey and Yarnold, Edward, SPCK, 1994, pp. 592–605.

29 Greene, Mark, *Thank God it's Monday*, Scripture Union, 1994, pp. 16, 17.

30 Sheppard, David, Allcock, James and Innes, Robert, *God at Work Part 2*, Grove Books, 1995, p. 15.

31 Niebuhr, *op. cit.*, p. 83.

32 *ibid.*, p. 41.

33 Rush, Myron, *Management: A biblical approach*, Victor Books, 1987, p. 7.

34 *ibid.*, p. 171.

35 Smith, Thomas, *God on the Job*, Paulist Press, 1995.

36 McGrath, Alister, *Roots That Refresh*.

37 *ibid.*, p. 146.

4 The Motivation to Work

1 Bridges, William, *op. cit.*, p. 37.

2 Statt, David A., *Psychology and the World of Work*, Macmillan, 1994, p. 111.

3 Drucker, Peter F., *Management*, Heinemann, 1988, p. 29.

4 Vroom, Victor H. and Deci, Edward L., *Management and Motivation*, Penguin, 2nd edn, 1992, p. 361.

5 McGregor, Douglas, *The Human Side of Enterprise*, McGraw-Hill, 1960, pp. 33, 34.

6 Kohn, Alfie, *Punished by Rewards*, Houghton Mifflin, 1993.

7 Graham, Pauline (ed.), *Mary Parker Follett – Prophet of Management*, Harvard Business School, 1995, p. 89.

8 McClelland, David C., *Human Motivation*, Cambridge University Press, 1987.

9 Maslow, Abraham H., *Motivation and Personality*, HarperCollins, 3rd edn, 1987.

10 *ibid.*, p. 3.

11 *ibid.*

12 *ibid.*, p. 22.

13 Chapter seven deals with this topic.

14 Maslow, Abraham H., *Motivation and Personality*, p. 251.

15 Herzberg, Frederick, *Work and the Nature of Man*, Staples Press, 1966, p. 71.

16 Schein, Edgar H., *Organizational Psychology*, Prentice-Hall, 3rd edn, 1988, p. 84.

17 Erikson, Erik, *Childhood and Society*, Triad/Granada, 1977, pp. 242–5 (*see* chapter seven of this book which describes Erikson's model).

18 Frank Lake adapted Erikson's model using the metaphor of a chair. Further details of Lake's work are available from Clinical Theology Association, St Mary's House, Church Westcote, Oxford OX7 6SF, England.

19 Fowler, James W., *Faith Development and Pastoral Care*, Fortress Press, 1987, pp. 53ff.

20 The copyright to the 16PF and 16PF5 is owned by the Institute for Personality and Ability Testing, Illinois. An excellent book is Cattell, Heather, *The 16PF: Personality in Depth*, IPAT, 1989.

21 MBTI and Myers Briggs Type Indicator are registered trademarks of Consulting Psychologists Press, Palo Alto, California, USA.

22 There is a substantial literature on the MBTI. Briggs Myers, Isabel, *Gifts Differing*, Consulting Psychologists Press, 1980, describes how it was developed and can be used. Helpful books by Christian writers include Goldsmith, Malcolm, *Knowing me Knowing God*, Triangle, SPCK, 1994; Goldsmith, Malcolm and Wharton, Martin, *Knowing me, Knowing you*, SPCK, 1993; Duncan, Bruce, *Pray Your Way*, Darton, Longman & Todd, 1993; Michael, Chester P. and Norrisey, Marie C., *Prayer and Temperament*, The Open Door, 1991.

23 Hebblethwaite, Margaret, *Finding God in All Things*, Fount, 1987.

24 *ibid.*, p. 29.

25 Wright, N. T., *The Epistles of Paul to the Colossians and to Philemon*, Inter-Varsity Press, 1986, pp. 149, 150.

5 Work: Choice or Calling?

1 Bonhoeffer, Dietrich, *Ethics*, Fontana, 1970, p. 254.

2 *ibid.*, p. 256.

3 *The Complete Works of St Teresa of Jesus*, Sheed & Ward, 1946, vol. 2, p. 71.

4 Leas, David, *On Marriage as Vocation*, Grove Books, 1996.

5 Bryant, Christopher, *The Heart in Pilgrimage*, Mowbray, 1994, pp. 88, 89.

6 *Alternative Service Book*, Central Board of Finance of the Church of England, 1980, pp. 345, 359.

7 Dewar, Francis, *Called or Collared*, SPCK, 1994, p. 8.

8 Motyer, J. A., *The Prophecy of Isaiah*, IVP, 1993, p. 380.

9 Walton, Steve, *A Call to Live*, Triangle, 1994.

10 Bonhoeffer, Dietrich, *op. cit.*, p. 257.

11 Walton, Steve, *op. cit.*, p. 25.

12 Scott Peck, M., *A. World Waiting To Be Born*, Arrow, 1993, p. 82.

13 Bridges, William, *Jobshift*, Nicholas Brealey Publishing, 1994.

14 Handy, Charles, *The Age of Unreason*, Business Books, 1989; *The Empty Raincoat*, Hutchinson, 1994.

15 Herriot, Peter, *The Career Management Challenge*, Sage, 1992.

16 Bolles, Richard N., *What Color is your Parachute?*, Ten Speed Press, 1995.

17 *ibid.*, p. 449.

18 Gardner, Howard, *Frames of Mind*, Fontana Press, 1993.

19 Illich, Ivan, *Deschooling Society*, Penguin, 1971.

20 Freire, Paulo, *Pedagogy of the Oppressed*, Penguin, 1969.

21 Payne, Leanne, *The Healing Presence*, Kingsway Publications, 1991, pp. 23ff.

22 Stokes, Andrew, *Working with God*, Mowbray, 1992, p. 50.

23 *ibid.*, p. 80.

24 Schumacher, Christian, *To Live and Work*, Marc Europe, 1987, pp. 102ff.

25 Temple, William, *Christianity and Social Order*, SPCK, 1976, p. 95.

26 *The Spiritual Exercises of St Ignatius*, Doubleday, 1964, p. 83.

27 *ibid.*, pp. 78ff.

6 Stress at Work

1 Fowler, H. W., *A Dictionary of Modern English Usage*, Oxford University Press, 1983, p. 593.

2 Jenkins, Rachel, 'Defining the Problem: Stress, Depression and Anxiety', *Promoting Mental Health Policies in the Workplace*, ed. Jenkins, Rachel and Warman, Dinah, HMSO, 1993.

3 *See*, for example, Cooper, Cary, Cooper, Rachel and Eaker, Lynn, *Living with Stress*, Penguin, 1988, pp. 14ff.

4 Described in Fontana, David, *Managing Stress*, Routledge, 1989, pp. 11ff.

5 Rahe, Richard, and Holmes, Thomas, 'The Social Readjustment Rating Scale', reproduced in Davies, Gaius, *Stress*, Kingsway Publications, 1988, p. 63.

6 Friedman, M. D., and Rosenbaum, R. H., 'A Predictive Study of Heart Disease', *Journal of the American Medical Association*, 189 (1964) pp. 15–22.

7 Kettle, Patsy, *Staying Sane Under Stress*, Grove Books, 1987.

8 *ibid.*, p. 24.

9 Davies, *op. cit.*, p. 40.

10 The Occupational Stress Indicator is published by NFER-NELSON Publishing Company.

11 Source unknown.

12 Foster, Richard, *Prayer*, Hodder & Stoughton, 1992.

13 de Mello, Anthony, *Sadhana, A Way to God*, Doubleday, 1978.

7 Identity, Self-Esteem and Work

1 Jacob, E., 'Psyche', *Theological Dictionary of the New Testament (abridged)*, ed. Kittel, Gerhard and Friedrick, Gerhard, abridged by Bromiley, Geoffrey W., The Paternoster Press, 1985, pp. 1342, 1343.

2 Russell, Bertrand, *History of Western Philosophy*, Routledge, 1991, p. 258.

3 Anderson, R. S., 'Self', *New Dictionary of Christian Ethics and Pastoral Theology*, ed. Atkinson, David J. and Field, David H., 1995, pp. 771, 772.

4 Ross, Warwick, 'Self', *A Dictionary of Pastoral Care*, ed. Campbell, Alistair V., SPCK, 1987, pp. 245, 246.

5 The Hebrew allows both translations.

6 St Augustine, *Confessions*, (first published AD 397), Folio Society, 1993, p. 13.

7 St Irenaeus, 'Adversus Haereses', in Bettenson, Henry, *The Early Christian Fathers*, Oxford University Press, 1969, p. 71.

8 Ward, Heather, *The Gift of Self*, Darton, Longman & Todd.

9 *ibid.*, p. 9.

10 *ibid.*, p. 10.

11 Bryant, Christopher, *The Heart in Pilgrimage*, Mowbray, 1994, p. 30.

12 Duncan, Bruce, *Pray your way*, Darton, Longman & Todd, 1993, p. 42.

13 Payne, Leanne, *The Healing Presence*, Kingsway, 1991, p. 48.

14 Duncan, Bruce, *op. cit.*, p. 42.

15 Harris, Thomas A., *I'm OK – You're OK*, Pan Books, 1973.

16 Erikson, Erik, *Childhood and Society*, Triad/Granada, 1977.

17 Capps, Donald, *Life Cycle Theory and Pastoral Care*, Fortress Press, 1983.

18 Fowler, James W., *Faith Development and Pastoral Care*, Fortress Press, 1987.

19 Jacobs, Michael, *The Presenting Past*, Open University Press, 1985.

20 Lake, Frank, *Personal Identity – Its Development*, Clinical Theology Association, 1987.

21 Erikson, Erik, *op. cit.*, p. 245.

22 McGrath, Joanna and McGrath, Alister, *The Dilemma of Self-Esteem*, Crossway Books, 1992, p. 34.

23 *ibid.*, p. 35.

24 Fromm, Erich, *To Have or To Be*, Abacus, 1979.

25 Neuro-Linguistic Programming is the 'study of subjective experience', the results of which have given birth to a variety of techniques aimed at enhancing well-being. The early classic study is by Bandler, R. and Grinder, J., *Frogs into Princes*, Real People Press, 1979. A recent introductory work is McDermott, Ian and O'Connor, Joseph, *Principles of NLP*, Thorsons, 1996. Some of the basic assumptions about human nature are at odds

with the biblical view (*see* pp. 143, 144 which set out some presuppositions).

26 *ibid.*, p. 41. *See also* chapter six in this book on the causes of stress.

27 An exception to this 'rule' is portrayed in Sheppard, Grace, *Pits and Pedestals*, Darton, Longman & Todd, 1995.

28 McGrath, Joanna and McGrath, Alister, *op. cit.*, pp. 51–6.

29 Lake, Frank, *Clinical Theology*, abridged by Yeomans, Martin H., Darton, Longman & Todd, 1986, pp. 29–37.

30 *ibid.*, p. 29.

31 Hoekema, Anthony A., *Created in God's Image*, The Paternoster Press, 1994, pp. 102–111.

32 Tournier, Paul, *The Meaning of Persons*, SCM Press, 1957, p. 232.

33 Satinover, Jeffrey, *The Empty Self*, Grove Books, 1995; Payne, Leanne, *op. cit.*, pp. 203ff.

34 Sheppard, Grace, *op. cit.*, p. ix.

8 Loss of Work

1 Handy, Charles, *The Empty Raincoat. Making sense of the future*, Hutchinson, 1994, p. 26.

2 Wiener, Norbert, *The Human Use of Human Beings*, Eyre & Spottiswoode, 1950, quoted by Sampson, Anthony, *Company Man*, HarperCollins, 1994, p. 186.

3 Pearson, Althea, *Growing through Loss and Grief*, Marshall Pickering, 1994, pp. 33, 34.

4 This pattern described is similar to that contained in the classic books on bereavement: Kubler-Ross, Elisabeth, *On Death and Dying*, Tavistock Publications, 1970; Parkes, Colin Murray, *Bereavement*, Tavistock Publications, 1972.

5 Worden, William J., *Grief Counselling and Grief Therapy*, Routledge, 1991, pp. 79ff.

6 Atkinson, David, *The Message of Job*, Inter-Varsity Press, 1991, p. 30.

7 Those concerned about using the psalms in this way might find

C. S. Lewis' book helpful, *Reflections on the Psalms*, Fontana, 1967, pp. 23ff.

8 Curran, Peter, *Coping with Redundancy*, CWR, 1995.

9 de Waal, Esther, *A World Made Whole*, Fount, 1991, p. 108.

9 Women and Work

1 de Beauvoir, Simone, *The Second Sex*, Pan Books, 1953.

2 Daly, Mary, *The Church and the Second Sex*, Geoffrey Chapman, 1968.

3 Moltmann-Wendel, Elisabeth and Moltmann, Jurgen, *God – his and hers*, SCM, 1991.

4 Harper, Michael, *Equal and Different*, Hodder & Stoughton, 1944, p. 131.

5 *ibid.*, p. 131.

6 Sayers, Dorothy L., *Unpopular Opinions*, Victor Gollancz, 1946, p. 106.

7 Stott, John R. W., *Issues Facing Christians Today*, Marshall Pickering, 1990, p. 258.

8 *See also* Banks, Robert, *God the Worker*, Albatross Books, 1992, pp. 123ff.

9 Henry, Matthew, *A Commentary on the Holy Bible*, Marshall Brothers, (first published 1700), vol. i, p. 12.

10 Kidner, Derek, *Genesis*, Tyndale Press, 1967, p. 71.

11 The ground is well covered in Stott, John R. W., *Issues facing Christians Today*, Marshall Pickering, 1990, pp. 254–84; ed. Lees, Shirley, *The Role of Women*, IVP, 1984, *passim*. Opposing views by evangelicals are contained in Harper, Michael, *Equal and Different*, Hodder & Stoughton, 1994; France, R. T., *Women in the Church's Ministry*, Paternoster Press, 1995.

12 Storkey, Elaine, *What's Right With Feminism*, SPCK, 1985, pp. 189ff.; Payne, Leanne, *The Healing Presence*, Kingsway, 1991, pp. 59ff.

13 Stott, *op. cit.*, p. 267.

14 Barrett, C. K., *A Commentary on the First Epistle to the Corinthians*,

A. & C. Black, 1971, p. 249.

15 Lincoln, Andrew T., *Ephesians*, Word Books, 1990, p. 388.

16 Field, David, 'Headship in marriage: the husband's view', Lees, Shirley, *op. cit.*, p. 55.

17 Sayers, *op. cit.*, pp. 109, 110.

18 *See* references under no. 11.

19 Sayers, *op. cit.*, p. 110.

20 Templeton, Elizabeth, ed., *A Woman's Place?*, Saint Andrew Press, 1993, p. 5.

21 Bowlby, John, *Child Care and the Growth of Love*, Penguin, 1953; Winnicott, D. W., *The Child, the Family and the Outside World*, Penguin, 1964.

22 Sylva, Kathy and Lunt, Ingrid, *Child Development*, Basil Blackwell, 1982.

23 Hillyer, Norman, *1 and 2 Peter, Jude*, Paternoster Press, 1992, p. 98.

24 Fordham, Frieda, *An Introduction To Jung's Psychology*, Penguin, 1966, p. 115.

25 Gill, Margaret, *Free to Love*, Marshall Pickering, 1994, pp. 2, 3.

26 Griffiths, Valerie, 'Mankind: male and female', Lees, Shirley, *op. cit.*, p. 78.

27 Borrowdale, Anne, *A Woman's Work*, SPCK, 1989, pp. 69ff.

28 Rogers, Carl, *On Becoming a Person*, Constable, 1967, p. 624.

29 Borrowdale, *op. cit.*, p. 72.

10 Providing Care

1 Coate, Mary Anne, *Clergy Stress*, SPCK, 1989.

2 Hurding, Roger F., 'Pastoral Care', *New Dictionary of Christian Ethics and Pastoral Theology*, ed. Atkinson, David J. and Field, David H., IVP, 1995, p. 78.

3 Campbell, Alistair V., 'Pastoral Care', *A Dictionary of Pastoral Care*, ed. Campbell, Alistair V., SPCK, 1987, p. 188.

4 Lake, Frank, *Clinical Theology*, abridged by Yeomans, Martin H., Darton, Longman & Todd, 1986, p. 14.

5 Dryden, Windy, Charles-Edwards, David, Woolfe, Ray, eds., *Handbook of Counselling in Britain*, 1989, pp. 134–59.

6 Taylor, Michael H., *Learning to Care*, SPCK, 1983, pp. 19–37.

7 Bridger, Francis and Atkinson, David, *Counselling in Context*, Marshall Pickering, 1994, pp. 31, 32.

8 Hurding, *op. cit.*, pp. 78–80.

9 Baxter, Richard, *The Reformed Pastor*, (first published 1656), Banner of Truth Trust, 1974, p. 66.

10 *ibid.*, p. 88.

11 Philip Doddridge's comment on Baxter's manual.

12 Campbell, Alastair, *Rediscovering Pastoral Care*, Darton, Longman & Todd, 1986.

13 *ibid.*, pp. 5, 82–97.

14 *The Alternative Service Book*, 1980, p. 145.

15 Dow, Graham, *op. cit.*, pp. 11–14.

16 Smith, Thomas, *God on The Job*, Paulist Press, 1995.

17 Baxter, Richard, *op. cit.*, p. 90.

18 *See*, for example, Cockerton, John, *Essentials of Evangelical Spirituality*, Grove Books, 1994, pp. 15, 16.

19 Greene, Mark, *op. cit.*, p. 15.

INDEX

The Divided Self

Closing the gap between belief and behaviour

Marlene Cohen

It's an age-old problem. 'I do not understand my own actions,' wrote St Paul. 'For I do not do what I want, but I do the very thing I hate.' Displaying a level of honesty that most of us would find difficult, he might as well have been speaking for the entire human race.

Yet it is easy to become sophisticated in disguising our less attractive, less acceptable selves, especially if we hold a position of leadership or trust.

This wise, honest and compassionate book explores the gap between professed belief and actual behaviour. Examining the sources of our belief systems, it offers a practical guide to the process of healing, integration and growth and is an essential guide both to understanding ourselves and others.

'No pastoral worker can afford to ignore the questions raised in this book'
Olive and John Drane

The Pastoral Encounter

Hidden depths in human contact

Brice Avery

This fascinating book takes readers of whatever counselling or pastoral persuasion on an intriguing journey through the backstreets of the city that is modern relational therapy. With insight, humour and material from his own casebook, psychiatrist Dr Brice Avery offers a practical understanding of the hidden factors that shape any pastoral encounter.

The first section of the book develops a Christian perspective on the determinants of individual identity and its implications for pastoral care. Section Two tackles the delicate process of making emotional contact with clients and yet retaining enough separateness to think and feel with objectivity. Finally, Brice Avery examines the part that spontaneity and ability play in forming the pastoral persona.

The Pastoral Encounter will fascinate and inspire pastoral carers whose training has given them an appreciation of the role of the unconscious in their work or who simply have an intuitive understanding of its importance.

Happy Families?
Building healthy families

John and Olive Drane

If family life is under attack, there seems to be no end of champions coming to its rescue: Church leaders, politicians, advertising gurus and media moguls are all busily promoting their own gospel of family values. Despite this, record levels of breakdown and divorce, with all their consequent trauma, indicate that the family as we know it clearly is in crisis.

What is at fault? In this groundbreaking book, John and Olive Drane find that many of our cherished notions of marriage and family life owe more to sentimentality than to biblical realism. This sensitive exploration of common problems that affect today's families, which brings to bear the Bible's emphasis on compassion, forgiveness and restoration, will be an indispensable aid to all in the pastoral and caring professions who help troubled families in their struggle towards freedom, grace and healing.

John Drane is a writer and theologian, and a gifted popular communicator. His previous books, *Evangelism for a New Age* and *What is the New Age Saying to the Church* are both published by Marshall Pickering.

For ten years, Olive Drane has been a chairperson of Children's Hearings (part of the Scottish legal system which deals with offences committed by and against children). She is also noted for her involvement with the arts in worship and evangelism.

John and Olive teach regularly together at Fuller Seminary, Pasadena, and are key speakers at Spring Harvest and similar events. They have been married for over 25 years and have three living children.